Embodying the Infinite
and
The Dissolution of the Separate Self

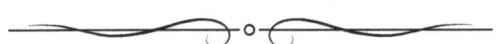

Stories, Transmissions, and Ancient Vedic Knowledge
for the Complete Liberation of Source Consciousness

JOI SHARP

Preface

There is an impulse within us. It is the impulse to grow beyond our individual perceived limitations and be free.

There is another impulse within us. It is the need to feel safe.

Both of these impulses can coexist simultaneously, yet they are independent. At any given time, one of these impulses has our attention. One is given more importance. Then, they may change places for a while and then change again.

These impulses are vital clues to a process we are cooperating with or a reality we are clinging to.

Which impulse is more vital? Which shall prevail?

This is our choice, and our capacity to choose is a gift.

Table of Contents

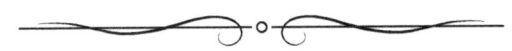

Introduction

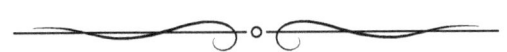

Just as the tree is contained in the seed,
and the butter pervades the milk,
God dwells in everything.

~Sri Mata Amritanandamayi Devi

This book is a prayer. It is a salutation to the Pure Consciousness that flows within all beings, the same Consciousness that blooms the flowers and moves the sun to rise every dawn. It is a prayer to a profound and powerful potential that can create, destroy, and connect with itself most profoundly and intimately.

This book recognizes a Universal Love that is pure Consciousness, a Love so powerful it can enter the darkest, scariest places within and completely change them into the purest Light. This book profoundly recognizes the Consciousness that resides within us all, the seed of infinite potential, the All that we are. This book is about the process of evolution latent within our physiology and our human species as consciousness. This process is a journey into discovering and exploring the ever-expanding field of Consciousness, which is the underlying reality everywhere and within everything.

In each of us, within our physical bodies, that field of consciousness is beginning to wake up, whether we are aware of it or not. Within this possible recognition lies the seed of infinite potential, just waiting for the right conditions to unfold. You and I, and all of humanity, are the containers of those conditions. The evolution of human consciousness is naturally unfolding, and just like any other process of evolution, significant and unforeseen changes are beginning to unfold.

The most important attitude is to stay open so that we may begin to sense an unimaginable intelligence within us. This intelligence has begun to unlock a design already in place. How we each relate to this "unlocking" affects our evolution. If we can take responsibility and care deeply for this new awakening, nurture it, and give it the space it needs, it will bloom. It is a new baby Buddha, and just like any newborn, it requires lots of attention and care.

We can call this process Spiritual. We might resonate with the word Spirit, another word for Consciousness. Other words we like might be Presence, God, the Light, Supreme Self, Atman, Brahmin or Soul. All these words can evoke a spiritual sense or feeling, but they all point to the same aliveness within us. In this book, I am using the word Consciousness because Consciousness is waking up in a conscious field; it is conscious of itself. Other words I use are the Divine, Infinite, Awareness and Totality.

This process will often feel "personal" as we continually encounter our limitations in the forms of insecurities, fears, judgments, and how we maintain our own "personal" isolation and separation.

At the core of this personal–felt process, we will experience our most significant and profound transformations as we begin to see that a "false self" is the source of the separation issues we experience. The "separate self" you have identified yourself with for your entire life is a false self, an entirely made-up self. From this made-up story, the vast field of Consciousness is waking up. When we see this for ourselves profoundly and objectively, it is called an Authentic Awakening. The infinite Consciousness no longer identifies itself as a small, separate self, and begins to unfold and mature within the physical body. This process of evolving and maturing can be incredibly inspiring or excruciatingly painful. It is this maturing process that this book is dedicated to. This process is spiritual, scientific, and extremely intimate, yet it cannot be explained away–it can only be traveled.

We are moving into a new life that leaves behind concepts and unfolds into a more sensing, intuitive life. Evolving consciousness is a matter of the heart, of deep devotion to that which is unfolding in this very moment, unfolding to include every fiber of our being. For some of us, the process is undeniable, and for some, it is more subtle. The change is felt within. The sense is that something extraordinary is happening, something that has never happened before. We might sense the profound realization that we have been drafted into this process, that it is not something we chose. We might deeply sense that this movement within us has an intelligence unfolding within our physical body, brain, and–the primary place that Consciousness opens this vessel–our nervous system.

We are leaving behind an old paradigm, one that has been centered on a dualistic reality. Consciousness is waking out of the Me Paradigm, thus dissolving the core of our separate existence. The old paradigm was about "me, myself, and I" being the center subject of existence and the subsequent identification with all the drama happening to "me." It was about "others" being everything other than "me, myself, and I." The old paradigm was about the "me" feeling separate and often extremely isolated—not connected to the fantastic, creative flow of Life. The "me" frequently felt victimized and frustrated by life because circumstances were not under "my" control.

These frustrations are evident in our society today, as our way of life has become wholly unsustainable. The desire to transcend insecurity by pretending that it doesn't exist has been our tendency, and often, we compensate by pretending to be strong rather than by looking deeply into the source of these feelings. But our deep-seated fears are still under the surface, feeding into the Me Paradigm, an illusion created from the belief that we are not enough or don't have enough. Perhaps we can use this old Me Paradigm as a springboard–by being aware of it– to dissolve our fears without too much struggle.

If our mind can understand the process of going beyond the Me Paradigm, it can begin to see where those fears are coming from, and we can begin to shift its identification. Our evolution is about becoming conscious–or Consciousness becoming conscious–and dissolving all identification with the Me Paradigm. The nature of consciousness is free of limitation, so naturally, any unconscious limitation within us will be exposed. This doesn't need to be difficult, but it will be if we want to believe it is difficult. If we attempt to talk ourselves out of fear (the "me" talking) or pretend it isn't there, that fear will not disappear. Maybe fear will hide for a while, deep in the unconscious, but it will return given the right circumstances. That tenacious fear is the foundation of the Me Paradigm.

As Consciousness evolves within us, we become more sensitive. We may intuitively sense that there is much more to know or experience. We are meant to live a more connected and whole life. We might become curious about what will become possible if we are no longer burdened with limiting beliefs and fears. Where is this curiosity coming from? What if we stay tuned to that small silent impulse urging us to keep going and being curious? The deeper we venture, the more we recognize that this process is not only for "us" but for the benefit of the entire creation. We are leaving the Me Paradigm.

For that to happen, there can be nothing in it for the "me." Personal illusions, or what the "me" wants, must dissolve completely before any new paradigm will reveal itself. We cannot imagine what the new paradigm will look like. The mind cannot know, yet it will try. We must enter the realm of the heart, where our true essence resides. Here, we will discover a different kind of security amid uncertainty- the uncertainty of the unknown. But with the Heart guiding the way, we will know what we are and how to live.

I am offering this little book to support you as a vessel for the evolution of consciousness. Within these pages are direct transmissions from my Guru, Mata Amritanandamayi, an authentic Divine incarnation, or great Mahatma. These transmissions are simple yet powerful in opening and exposing personal illusions. I offer these gifts with complete humility, just as they were given to me. We are fellow travelers—continually discovering how the Infinite wants to live. I found many illusions in myself that we all share, many of which were quite subtle. We, as a species, share the experience of evolution. Some folks will embrace it, and others will not, but either way, evolution is happening. I am including in this book some stories about my time with Amma. These stories are only a tiny fraction of the many transformative situations I experienced, and I got to know their familiar flavor as directly linked to the Satguru. There is no possible way I could include them all, but they all had the same effect- dissolving the false, separate self within me. They are very precious memories, even the most difficult ones! Yet even more important are their teachings. A true Master teaches through example, and Amma is amazingly effective. And so, I am also including these stories to show how a real Sat-Guru works–deep within, creating the circumstances to expose every remaining strand of ignorance.

Many people misunderstand the idea of having a true Master. If you are one of these folks, I invite you to question where your beliefs come from. Having a guru/disciple relationship isn't for everyone, and unless you meet your eternal guru, you simply have not met Her/Him. If you meet your guru, you will know it immediately, and if you are wise, you will recognize that the relationship is eternal. For my journey, having Amma in my life has been essential, and our relationship continues to inspire me—as a vessel—to keep opening to Love. I have always known that Amma has taken my most sincere desire for complete Self-realization seriously. She also doesn't allow me to settle for anything less. She nudges, guides, supports, and inspires the most profound process to take place within. She knows what she is doing. The evolutionary process is naturally different for each person. My journey will not look like yours, and yours will not look like anyone else's. Yet we all share the same field of consciousness, awakening, so naturally, there will be many similarities.

As you read, feel free to use what resonates with you, and know that if something doesn't resonate, it doesn't mean it is wrong. Know that some of what I speak of may be experienced differently and at different times by different people. You might never experience some of what I speak of, and that's okay, too. Throughout this process, I invite you to give any resistance a chance; sometimes, what we resist might be the perfect thing we need to hear.

This book is an offering in the most profound sense. This book is a tool to help you keep your mind open and receptive so that Consciousness can be free to expand and mature within. My words are not the truth since no words possibly could be. They point to what cannot be spoken of but that lies within you and all creation. I sincerely hope that you use these pointers openly as a beginner so that the "knower" can be out of the way, and you receive the direct transmission that these words carry. These words can enter your being if you allow them and deliver a direct experience. The transmission is coming from the Light of Consciousness into consciousness. The words come from experience; they are not merely concepts. As we enter the realms of the most profound surrender, we will lose our capacity to hold onto concepts, and it becomes necessary to discard them. There may be places in the book where I repeat myself; if you can stay open, the repetition can get in. You may encounter para-doxes, and it may sound like I contradict myself sometimes because the words are only relevant in how they are pointing. The words come from a living, breathing presence, and I am offering them so that they may touch that same presence in you.

1.

Cooperating with the Inevitable

Once we accept our limits, we go beyond them.

~Albert Einstein

*I*t's about 4 am, and the night birds are still out calling in the high canopies of the coconut palms. The stars twinkle through the broad leaves above, and the air is just slightly cool compared to the hot daytime humidity. This rural coastal rainforest has an uncanny stillness, and the felt sense of presence is all around.

I am standing with several others in the open sandy yard behind Amma's ashram in Kerala, India. We are gathered around, looking at a seating chart taped to the side of a bus, standing among two other buses as ashram residents loaded pots, boxes, and luggage and strap them to the tops. We are about to embark on a seven-week tour of North India. The year is 1995, and this will be my first North India tour, which I have heard about for a couple of years and have resisted going. I had heard how wonderful the tour could be, how tough it was, and how full of intense tapas (challenges designed to take you beyond your comfort zone), and last year, I knew I wasn't ready for intense tapas.

However, this year, I signed up. Others have told me that on tour, we get to be with Amma on the road, and every day, we have regular stops with her to go swimming, eat our meals, and meditate out in nature. But now, the reality of committing to this venture is catching up. I feel like I am entering Goddess Kali's domain, and I am scared. The seating chart says that I am assigned to a seat in the last row in a three-seater, and I am in the middle. I feel an intense anxiety creep in, and my mind says that this seating arrangement is going to be impossible. For the record, I am a Colorado girl with red hair and an extremely sensitive disposition that gets hot very quickly. I am used to wide-open mountain spaces with cool air and very few people around.

Since I arrived in India last year, I have felt emotionally fragile, and my body's intense sensitivity has gone through the roof. How in Amma's name was I going to be able to endure a seven-week tour riding in the heat of India squished in the back of the bus between two strangers? Maybe I should not go; perhaps I should stay in the ashram, go into silence, and meditate like I did last year. That was such a lovely, peaceful time, and to go deep inside was good for my spiritual growth. But then I realized I couldn't back out; my luggage was already on top of the bus, buried somewhere in that mountain of bags tied down, all nice and secure. Almost everything I have is in that bag, and I know I need to go on this tour. I step up onto the bus. I have already done a few shorter tours, a one-day bus ride to a program and then back to the ashram, so I know what to expect.

Packed boxes and big cooking pots fill the aisles, where the young Indian Brahmacharinis (women monks) will ride. How they do this is a fantastic feat. I carefully make my way over the obstacles towards the back of the bus, my eyes dialing in on my seat. I slip in as I am still waiting for my seatmates to arrive. The seat is a hard vinyl bench with a hardback. It would be narrow even for two people, and there are supposed to be three of us? The space where our feet are supposed to go has boxes wedged tight, so there is no place to put *your feet, and you must rest them on top of the boxes with your knees drawn up. How is this possible? This isn't going to be good for my sensitive body at all! As I look around, I see that all the spaces in front of the seats have boxes. Maybe we can move around once the tour starts, like on a plane…*

The bus fills up with the ashram residents, and I can sense everyone's nervous excitement. No, I am not the only one who knows in my heart that we are about to drive to our deaths. My seatmates find their way back, and we all exchange nervous smiles as we wedge in our wide Western hips. We are squeezed in against each other, with me in the middle, making me cringe as I have a solid repulsion for physical contact these days. Immediately, an overpowering grip of claustrophobia and panic takes over…. Oh my God! What am I doing? I cannot do this…Amma, get me out of here! I gotta get off the bus NOW!

There is an audible hush throughout the bus, and all heads are turned as one towards the front. Amma has just come on the bus! She is coming to check on us. She is all 4'8" of smiles and tenderness. I feel the tears well up, and an overpowering Love rises in my heart. Oh, Amma, how can I survive this? Amma looks straight at me, way in the back. She holds my gaze for a long, long time. There is neither a look of Love nor tenderness; instead, she looks at me with a powerful knowing. I know she sees right through me, feeling all my terror. I can feel her give me a deep transmission; I know I must go through this. Amma is right here with me. I must go, and I sense that this is a process to get over some deep conditioning of my ego. But I don't want to go; I want to be comfortable. The buses start their engines, and Amma gets off to get into her car. My bus mates start chanting the Sri Lalita Sahasranama, the thousand names of the Divine Mother, and the buses pull out of the yard onto the road through the sleeping village. There is a feeling of determination in the sound of the bus itself; the engine sounds like God is in charge. I feel the invitation to let go to that power, that the journey will do the work. I just need to get on the bus and stay on the bus.

2.

The False, Separate self

~~~~~~~~~~

When the sense of "I" and "me" fades away,
the pure Atman will awaken.

~Omkara Divya Porule V52, Amrita Gita

Have you ever felt that you were very different from everyone around you? Of course, you did because of the nature of duality or "otherness." When you were younger, did you feel overly sensitive and wish to be like everyone else? Did you long to fit in? I remember being sensitive when I was a kid and hating it; I wanted to feel normal and be like everyone else. At the same time, I would feel quite empathic when others were hurting; it was as if I could feel their pain intensely, and this made me uncomfortable. I didn't like feeling so vulnerable with others around me because it made me feel out of control. And it made me feel awkward.

Little did I know that those initial, intense feelings of being different were the beginning of my spiritual journey. As a child, consciousness was already going into the density of separation within me and bringing it to a conscious level. My life ever since has been a gradual whittling away of the roots of separation. This wasn't done through any remarkable enlightenment experience. The dissolution of separation is taking place because my life has presented me with the perfect circumstances for it to happen, all on its own. The separation was always in me, as a vast network of neurological programs created from my past and my past lives. Through my process, I now see my perceived sense of separation was never actual or concrete, even though the whittling away of my sense of separation has felt very real. However, because the mind-body complex was identified with the experience of separation, it created a reality I have lived in. You have probably experienced a similar sense of separation as I have.

We all know what it is like to feel like a separate self and all the quirkiness that can come with that experience. One of the first things that comes to mind is the myriad of feelings around insecurity and fear. The false self constantly thinks about its future, striving towards a day when it feels completely secure and happy. There may be desires that create an imagined feeling of happiness if fulfilled. The false self will continually attempt to maintain a good image for others, covering up and avoiding any feelings of insecurity. The false, separate self tends to resist uncomfortable emotions, as it identifies with them and then judges them as weaknesses, believing something is "wrong." This further entangles the complicated knot of a false identity.

The separate self continually harbors hopes about its future or regrets from the past, unable to live a spontaneous, authentic life. The separate self often experiences daily life through layers of unconscious beliefs and interpretations. And when we—as separate selves – believe those beliefs, we cannot free ourselves from the knot that binds us. We then become limited by what we think and feel, and we experience life as something that happens to "us." In other words, the false, separate self is a big knot of entanglement, susceptible to the winds of change.

The separate self might imagine how it can transcend those feelings of separation and isolation. It dreams of itself as a better, separate self that is significant and loved by all. The separate self looks to the world for these improvements and to the world to define who it is as a person. The separate self has a codependent relationship with the world and needs the world to validate itself. Most of the time, the drives of the separate self to feel better about itself are deeply hidden within the unconscious, leaving many of the root causes of separation hidden. True spirituality is about exposing our hidden core stories, which we inherited as children and perhaps in previous births. These core beliefs are the programs causing us to believe that we are a separate, isolated self. Most of these beliefs contribute to feelings of lack and inadequacy, which is why we look to the world to fill those feelings of emptiness.

The separate self is a created illusion, a fabricated story of thoughts, beliefs, and self-images, all of which reside in our neurological memories. These unconscious programs create a dense identification with the body. This identification is an aspect of ego that creates the illusion of "others."

This self was created when our brain learned it was a "me." It was created by our environment when we were children and all the many ways the brain learned to relate to itself as a "me." These conditioned tendencies are also what we brought with us in the subtle body from past lives.

When we begin looking at this illusion, encountering endless emotions and layers of mental conditioning, it may seem too monumental a task to dismantle. The false self doesn't want to dismantle itself and might project onto a too painful or complicated task. The false self will judge anything negative that it encounters about itself, such as emotions or habits, entangling the illusion even further. The false self is unconsciously insecure, so anything seen as unfavorable will feed that insecurity. Since the false self is nothing more than hard-wired programs in the brain, it is a habit that will do anything to hold onto what it knows. It will fight to stay in its rigid perceptions and behaviors.

The false, separate self is borne through its core story or beliefs about itself. It is an entanglement of neurological psychology. Most of this entanglement, like programs from the past, resides in the subconscious. Every false self has a core story around insecurity and lack, but many cannot recognize this because the brain keeps things hidden. The core story keeps the separate self behaving the way it does, for the story is the creator of the separate self. Knowing your core story can be very helpful. Tuning into the core story of the body/mind complex can reveal a deep, emotional root cause of separation.

If not seen objectively, the separate self can feel horrified by its core story. The false self's unconscious tendency to not want to know the story might come back into play, and the insecurity goes unconscious again. So, the real opportunity is to see that the separate self and its core story are essentially innocent, and this is done in the light of pure Awareness. Here are some typical stories the separate self operates out of; see if any of these feel familiar in your body/mind.

"Nobody understands me."

"People always leave/abandon me."

"I'll never get it right."

"I am not lovable or worthy of Love."

Etc...

Some separate selves adopt more "egoic" beliefs to cover up their core stories, such as "I know," "I am so evolved," etc. But these beliefs cover up the deeper core story/separate self, hiding the feelings of insecurity and lack. Core stories can become even more "unhealthy," but if you keep looking objectively, most people will have one of these at the core. These "core wound stories" are simply a way for the mind to understand relationships or situations. The brain only wants to understand things, so it takes any information from the past and creates stories or understandings. These understandings help the brain feel like it's in control, to keep the mind-body safe.

It's also, indirectly, a way to protect the separate self from dissolution. And this is where the entanglement of the separate self begins- in the need to stay safe.

My core story is a slight variant of "Nobody understands me." I have seen in myself a particular, energetic tug that becomes very familiar when my story kicks in. I have watched my whole being turn away from someone like it is being controlled through an inner program, and that is precisely what a core story is: It's an inner program. I remember sitting next to someone once, and the thought came in, "he doesn't understand me." It was a thought with such conviction that my whole being believed it. My body turned away, and I saw the genesis of separation in my body/mind. All the neurological pathways fired together to maintain that belief. But gradually, through time, every time the story kicked in, I could see it and allow that insecure part of me to be there in the Light of Awareness, and it gradually faded away.

Looking at the automatic reactions, through thoughts and feelings, when certain situations present themselves, you can see some that emerge from the core story. Our way of responding to situations can be traced back to our core story. Our reactions can support and perpetuate the story, so it is a re-action. It is our way of repeatedly reacting to a specific situation because of the unconscious core story that feeds it. The core story can also cause us to grasp onto something or someone, needing to fill that sense of lack. In other words, if my story is "no one understands me," my brain might create behaviors that need to be understood or heard. Interestingly, this is more of a co-dependent tendency, and we see it often in spiritual circles.

An attitude of curiosity can be constructive when looking at our core stories. In a moment of grace, a space opens up. The light of consciousness shines on our core story; we will recognize it has been with us our entire lives. We will see that it has governed our very existence. Seeing the story objectively is essential. The false self can become highly agitated by its story, even though it hides within it. The false self *is* the story. It doesn't want to see its scarcity and incompleteness. It will judge its story and attempt to avoid it. I have witnessed the false self attempt to cover up its story by acting solid and sure of itself. When I saw this, I recognized its familiarity as a learned pattern in the brain. But trying to act confident and strong when insecurity is underneath is just repression, which can cause a whole other mess of things to deal with.

Seeing from Awareness is a natural aspect of consciousness. We are, simply put, what "sees, or observes." We are the Awareness that sees. When actual seeing occurs, it is unbiased. It is entirely free of agenda, meaning we are not trying to eliminate anything. We are not trying to change anything. However, identification with what we are seeing may arise in the initial seeing. Allow it to arise. Let it all come up. In the Light of Awareness, we allow everything. Don't dismiss it or bypass the identification. It needs to be exposed in its entirety.

We are the light, and the light dispels illusion. The more we see, the more we know we are that which sees, and the firmer and more rooted in conscious Awareness our new perspectives become. Seeing becomes increasingly more precise. We are not creating a new identification for ourselves; it is a relinquishing of identification. We are halting the need to be anything at all.

The more we see, the more we want to see. This is consciousness freeing itself. We are not trying to attain anything or maintain any state. The seeing through of illusion—the false, separate self—is an incredibly freeing experience. But we don't dismiss any part of this self—that would be spiritual bypassing. We must enter it and infuse it with consciousness. We must acknowledge its unconscious needs and wants so that all these parts of the self can relax. This is all that is needed for the deepest healing of our lives. Acknowledge and allow so that the brain's false identity feels safe. And that is all that is needed. Allowing from conscious Awareness is an alchemical approach of deep integration and healing. The integration of self allows relaxation that culminates in dissolution because all the behaviors and beliefs are not needed anymore. But this process takes tremendous patience, devotion, and time—lots of it. But what else are we here for?

3.
Awakening

Once you go beyond the ego, you are nothing. Y
ou are infinite nothingness, filled with Divine Consciousness.

~Sri Mata Amritanandamayi Devi

Our spiritual process is the impulse that originates from the vast field of consciousness—to wake up from the false identification as a separate person. It is a process that removes all the perceptions of "I" and "mine." In the ancient Vedic texts, these perceptions are known as "ignorance." To know who we are, ignorance must be removed.

The ancient philosophy of Sanatana Dharma, which is the root of many other religions, teaches us how to live. Vedanta's essential guidance is contained within its vast texts. Remove the ignorance of the mind to know the truth of who you are- as the Universal Self or Cosmic Consciousness.

Our mind's latent tendencies, often buried deep within the unconscious, create these illusions of separation. Vasanas are all the habitual, unconscious ways we live, our mental conditioning, likes, dislikes, and all the ways we remain convinced that this world is real. These *vasanas* are frequently quite subtle, requiring the guidance of a real master to expose them through circumstances designed just for this purpose. It is often a bit painful, as all our identification with these tendencies shows up. It's not the *vasanas* that cause the pain but rather our identification with them. This is the separate self, and removing the identification so that the vasanas can be transformed is the process.

This evolutionary process is never about becoming a better or nicer separate self, although this is often a byproduct. It is about dissolving by seeing through the unconscious programs of the separate self. Life is here to expose those programs so that consciousness awakens from its small and narrow experience of itself and becomes free.

In the moment consciousness awakens from the limited identification as a separate self, that separate self ceases to exist. This happens all the time to everyone, but most people have no idea where that fresh sense of ease came from. When we are in awe of a sunset or the thrill of an experience, we forget ourselves because our perceptions shift from the habituated separation programs. We feel free. This is why many people repeatedly look for those experiences–maybe through an extreme outdoor activity or dancing ecstatically–but we know those experiences don't last. The habituated perceptions come back. In the next moment, the identity as a separate self resurrects, and consciousness again feels separate.

But when the time is ripe and the soul is ready, the pure, unconditioned Awareness of consciousness begins to recognize the separate self through its neurological and psychological make-up. When we encounter our emotions or thoughts, conscious Awareness feels and sees them. If there is enough openness within us, the light of consciousness can penetrate the entanglement of the separate self. This pure Consciousness emerges from the entanglement, beginning to free itself from the knots of identification.

Awakenings are not necessarily big events, as they will suit each person according to their needs. In the beginning, awakenings may seem big, but gradually, they become more subtle and accumulative. Awakening becomes normalized if we remain open and not get in our own way. In this way, something magical begins to happen. Continuous shifts can accumulate even without our participation, which is interesting because then there is no identity whatsoever. We are no longer looking for that constant great experience because we are free of the need for that. The shifts only happen to consciousness, from consciousness.

The separate self loves super special stuff, so as consciousness dissolves identification as a self, extraordinary experiences aren't that special to us anymore (even though they continue to happen). What we are looking for isn't an experience. What we are looking for is freedom from false identification. This is true liberation from the separate self, and once we get a taste of real freedom, we move towards deepening that freedom.

As consciousness frees itself from the roots of separation, we can feel incredibly liberated, especially at first. We have more spaciousness within, and conscious Awareness is less restricted. Consciousness is beginning to free itself of perceived limitations, and we have more space to see more.

The most common shifts are the temporary shifts, where we awaken out of the false self by seeing that it is not what we are but rather its self-created illusion from all our past programs. This kind of shift can be incredibly wonderful, especially if the separate self has suffered a lot. The separate self will continue to come back in, either immediately or after some time, but conscious Awareness has recognized it, and there is now a crack that the light can get in to see more.

We must remember that this is a process, not an end. Past programs run very deep. We are uncovering generations and lifetimes of trauma, experiences, and beliefs. But this is not digging into the past. It is being open to the present.

I have seen many people get frustrated because they get sucked back into that old, contracted selfdom after experiencing a vast new view. Some folks call this "I got it, I lost it." It usually just means that consciousness is now penetrating a new layer of illusion. We can never lose who we are, but we might think we "lost it" when our identity shifts back to the separate self. This, too, can be revealing, as the separate self gets frustrated as it reencounters its old tight experience. The separate self wants out of its experience of itself but wants to keep its wonderful new experience of the vast view. So, this "I got it, I lost it" has an intelligent way of dissolving any tendency towards ownership of a shift. The separate self has a highly complex drive to hang on to anything good, so we welcome whatever it takes to dissolve those tendencies. Recognize that when there is a temporary shift, and we find ourselves back in a tight, contracted perspective, it is only a sense of tightness. We might find ourselves in identification, which may take a little while to see. Yet, conscious awareness means awareness of the contraction, and we can stay open even to the contraction. We can allow ourselves to be where we are.

Consciousness is waking up in its organic way. If we want an awakening "back," just the simple desire to have it back closes things up again and blocks a natural process from happening. If we stay open and honest with our experience in this present moment, then we are aligned with our evolutionary process. We can sense the invitation to relax even in confusion and lack of clarity.

Awakening is a shift that opens a doorway, and with it comes a lot of responsibility. It can be any ordinary life circumstance that opens that door. There are no better ways and no right ways. It is up to us to keep that opening free from personal agenda. If we do not continue to nourish that opening through genuine devotion and integrity, it will close all on its own, and we might be so asleep that we will convince ourselves that the doorway is still open. I have seen this happen in folks who were very sincere in their spiritual process. The door closed because of the insecurity of the separate self, which developed a new agenda.

After an initial Awakening, the separate self will still have all its latent tendencies, which feed its insecurity. And so, it comes back and may want the awakening to become a new version of itself. The separate self is incomplete, so it will look for anything to make itself feel complete. The separate self needs to feel good about itself- that is its drive. An awakened separate self is a tricky way to cover up the incompleteness. A false sense of completeness can exist even with lots of unconscious insecurity, so be aware. I have seen this happen and have watched people take their initial awakening to create a newly awakened ego-self, which shuts the door to any new shifting. Eventually, however, the light of consciousness will get through in its own time and way.

The personal aspect of the separate self can come in and "own" the awakening. But in a few rare people, the personal aspect falls away as consciousness matures in the mind-body, and the threat of them owning the shift is absent. The separate self is still there, but the threat of feeling special about itself is gone. This is a huge blessing of grace, allowing the aspirant to mature as a conscious awareness. There is simply not enough of the personal aspect to have an "awakened self." Many people have awakening experiences, yet for most folks, the personal aspect hasn't dissolved from their system. And when they make it "my awakening," the sense of ownership has come from the personal aspect of the separate self.

When the personal aspect of the separate self dissolves completely, we lose our capacity to self-assess. We can't wonder about how we are doing or where we are in "our" process. We no longer have any ability to maintain any image of ourselves. I have seen a funny attempt at creating an image in myself as a thought—like maybe I should act differently, but to go through with it is impossible. When the personal aspect is absent, we can sense that something is *very* different in how we relate to the world, but because we have lost that ability to self-assess, we can't recognize what it is. Sometimes, the individual doesn't know that a significant shift has occurred because of this inability to self-assess. It can be an odd place for a while. The individual senses that she comes from a different place than most people. In this shift, the possibility of the separate self owning the awakening isn't there, but the chance of getting stuck still is. Getting stuck can occur when the separate self "likes" the new space it finds itself in. The term "drunk on emptiness" applies here, and if we are not under the watchful eyes of a proper guide, we can get stuck here for a long, long time. It is a helpful place to rest, and that's fine. It's almost beneficial to allow the body-mind to get accustomed to the absence of a personal self, as it can initially feel disorienting. But if we want to evolve as consciousness, nurturing of the opening must continue. If we are honest with ourselves, we can sense that we are not "done" and that there is much more to see.

You may be trying to figure out if you have lost part of the self and if you are now awake. This is understandable, yet it is all meaningless because there is always more to see, and the deeper we go, the more constant the seeing will become. If we remain open to our process, we will begin to recognize a profound maturing, a process of being embodied by consciousness. This recognition gives our body-mind a deep sense of satisfaction because this is what it was made for.

The only reason I mention these different ways the separate self can block the awakening process is so your mind can begin to become aware of them. The separate self misinforms the mind, so when a deep embodiment of consciousness begins to occur, the mind can also begin to awaken and reflect what is true. The mind gets on board with this process of being embodied rather than "awakened." Through the embodiment process, the mind becomes purified and transformed. The source of the mind is the pure light of consciousness, expansive and boundless, and awakening opens the door for the mind to have a completely different function.

This is only the beginning of our embodiment process. In these initial phases, diligence and devotion are essential. We might feel such relief from an initial shift that we could easily miss that there is more to see. A lot more. We are not free of feeling separate- consciousness has merely seen through it and opened itself up. The separate self is not gone; it has only been seen through for a moment (hours or days). All those unconscious habitual programs are still there, just under the surface.

If the personal aspect has fallen away, insecurity and fear can still reside in the unconscious. There is still a separate self, and all the latent neurological tendencies will be reflected in the mind. The excellent news is that consciousness will use all these tendencies to become more aware of itself. When we see insecurity within our being, we mustn't dismiss it, as this quickly falls into repression and bypassing. The separate self in the form of insecurity often hides, and when we see it, it needs to be acknowledged and allowed. Pure Conscious Awareness has no judgment about insecurity. When we see it, we see it as a natural aspect of a separate self. Acknowledgment and allowance are the natural response to clear seeing. Naturally, a self that believes it is separate will be insecure. It only wants to feel safe. Separation fosters insecurity. We can see examples of this everywhere.

When we become familiar with the feeling of the insecure self, we can be attentive to it when it arises. It feels separate and unsafe, and the more we recognize it, the more we will be aware of it even when it is not arising. It is merely a part of the mind-body complex. As Awareness strengthens and matures, the seeing will become more robust and precise. This seeing dissolves the separate self through allowing, as unconditioned Awareness is the magical alchemist. If there is judgment towards the separate self, it comes from that self. Consciousness Awareness does not judge; it allows.

Curiosity keeps us open and objective. The discovery of the separate self is a natural evolutionary step. This process has many phases; they are all essential. If we remain open, we may experience many shifts or awakenings. Most of these shifts will be subtle, as most of the separate self's tendencies are hidden from our everyday view. The accumulation of these small, subtle shifts can profoundly transform us and help us develop a mature perspective. They make us strong and resilient. This mature perspective completely cooperates with the organic process as it unfolds, as maturity comes from the Supreme Self.

The process of evolution is not a linear advancement, although there are phases that we will all go through. The process is happening right now—only right now. The function of the light of consciousness is to dissolve illusions and evolve by becoming conscious of itself. To wonder where we are along the journey is entirely extraneous. This kind of self-assessing will only come from the separate self…yes…it's still with us. Yet, if we remain conscious of this ignorance, life will take care of everything else.

This is how devotion can greatly assist us if we genuinely want liberation. We stay open to the fact that we are not done, and the Great Mystery beckons us further. A real Master can see the unconscious tendencies and create the right circumstances to show us where the separate self lies hidden. I am forever grateful to Amma for this assurance, as I recognize that I could not have traversed these pitfalls without her. The pure awareness that perceives the separate self's profound subtleties is the Sat guru's awareness. This level of Awareness is the true Self, the eternal Being that is always here.

4.
A Swimming Lesson

When the storm brews and the waves swell,
only an experienced captain can control the ship.

~Sri Mata Amritanandamayi Devi

1995. We are on the road in India, and it is unbelievably hot. The buses have become a moving sweatbox with all of us squeezed together. An odd assortment of bags and scarves hang overhead, swaying to the movement of the bus. Everyone is quiet, as it makes us hotter just to speak.

But we all know we are about to get a break, as we are being led by Amma's car, and she is looking for a good place for us to swim. One of the highlights of each day is getting to "swim" with Amma. I wouldn't call it swimming, although sometimes we do swim. It is more like we get in a river or a lake and get wet…with Amma. Amma plays with us, and we chant the Gayatri mantra, blessing the river with sacred sounds. Afterward, the sweltering stickiness of the day is replaced by the incredible, refreshing experience of our time with Amma. We are renewed and revived. It's the best.

The girls get to swim in an ashram-styled "swim dress." These dresses are not the best for swimming, as they consist of a large fabric billowing down to mid-calf, held up by an elastic band around the upper chest and two wide shoulder straps. It's almost dangerous to try and swim in these dresses. The boys wear a short cloth folded above their knees and tied around their waist.

Finally, the buses turn off, and we arrive at our swimming spot. All of us step out of the bus. We are at a small river in a quiet rural area. There are lovely big trees overhead and plenty of shade. I go down to the river to a secluded spot where I don't see anyone else. I am doing this because it is my menses time, and tradition dictates that women should stay away from Amma during this time. We are told this is for our benefit, as being close to Amma affects our cycle. I am trying to do what I should, so I head to where I know I can be alone and still cool off.

I step into the water, which is not the cleanest but wet and cool. Suddenly, I hear a familiar laugh, and, turning around, I see Amma! Oh no! She is approaching me with a couple of Brahmacharis (male monks). She looks at me and laughs again, and I know I cannot stay away from Amma much longer.

Amma comes closer to me in a very playful mood. The boys are laughing. She comes and stands right in front of me, says something in Malayalam, and points to me and her shoulders. There is a look of dismay on the boys' faces as it becomes clear that Amma wants me to get on her shoulders! Now, you must understand that I am a good foot taller than Amma, and even though I am slender, I still weigh a substantial amount. The boys shake their heads, signaling I will NOT get on Amma's shoulders. Again, Amma interrupts and points to me and her shoulders, stressing that she wants me to get on them! What am I to do? I shake my head and tell her no. Please, Amma, I can't do that. Please Amma. No. Don't make me do that!

Amma lets out an exasperated sound and dives under the water behind me. Suddenly, I feel her head pushing between my legs from behind! Oh no! Then I rise out of the water as Amma stands up, with me perched on *her shoulders, straddling her head! The look on the boys' faces is one of horror as they take in the sight. I feel ashamed- they are going to blame me for this enactment. Amma just laughs as she struts around with her prize perched precariously where she knows I cannot get away. I can't believe this is happening…OMG! Suddenly, Amma laughs in glee and throws me backward in the water! I simultaneously feel horrified and relieved but do not want to face those boys. I come up for air, and the look they give me shows they blame me for this incident. They have no idea that I only wanted to stay away from Amma. Culturally, we are from different planets, so approaching them and explaining myself would be a traditional no-no. Meanwhile, Amma is already walking away toward the next delightful play she can instigate.*

I felt that Amma knew the programming of my need to do things "right" and my tendency towards perfectionism. After this incident, she started to show me that I needed to lighten up a bit. Amma gave me one of the most delightful memories of my time with her. She created a situation to break that "good girl" tendency, and she did it in a way that was so beautiful and full of Love.

There was another similar circumstance soon after that. It was also a swimming day. Again, I was trying to stay away from Amma, but she created a situation where I was literally at her feet for a long time. There was nothing I could do to get up! I found myself in heaven, resting my head on her feet. My beloved Mother was showing me the freedom to let go of what I was told was correct and to go with the flow, which ended up being a huge blessing. The need to do things right in a traditional setting can be very sticky, and the mind can rigidly interpret rules. I found myself in a very different tradition in

Southern India. My mind interpreted the tradition according to its understanding (of which it had none). So, I adopted a reasonably rigid persona, completely blocking my playfulness and spontaneity. Many folks find themselves in a traditional setting and adopt the ways of the tradition but interpret them in a fixed and rigid way, which can block a person's spiritual unfolding. Amma saw this tendency in me and began to set it free.

5.
The Experience of Now

The foundation of spirituality is not blind faith.
It is inquiry; it is an intense exploration within one's self.

~Sri Mata Amritanandamayi Devi

1999. Here I am, just back from India. Some friends here in Western Colorado have been nice enough to let me stay with them until I can get a job and make money to return to Amritapuri Ashram. I am exhausted from the long flight, and my heart breaks from leaving Amma's physical presence. I am trying to appear normal but feel like a fish out of water—I feel disconnected here. My friends have no idea what I have been through in India; it has been a very tough year of intense de-conditioning while in Amma's presence. I wonder if I seem weird to them. I feel weird. I know it is because I am so sensitive. So, I will attempt to act "normal" for their sake. Everything will be okay if I can convince others that I am OK.

It is snowing outside, even though it is April. It usually takes me about a week to feel like my sleep patterns are back on track, so every morning, I feel out of it. This morning, my friend, whom I'll call Alice, comes into the kitchen and tells me that I will have to leave, that it will not work out for me to stay with them.

I feel like I have been given an eviction notice, and my world unravels. "When do you want me out?" I ask.

"Today, get your things together, and I will give you a ride to Telluride, where you can look for a job," she says.

I tell her that it is snowing out, and because it is April, there are no jobs—it is off-season, and during off-season, everyone vacates the town. And if it is snowing here at 5,000 feet in elevation, it will be dumping and freezing at 9,000 feet, which is the elevation of Telluride. Oh, and of course, there is the fact that I have nowhere to stay up there.

Alice tells me that this is not her concern. I must point out that Alice is also a devotee, and I have always thought of her as family. We've known each other for about three years and have never had any difficulty. But she has never been to India and isn't aware of the challenge of going back and forth. So, I ask her why she wants me to leave, and she says that now is not a good time. I'm surprised; her spacious country house has two extra bedrooms.

So, I call up an acquaintance, a friend named Joe, who lives in Telluride, and he tells me he is house-sitting a big estate outside of Telluride, and I can stay in his room in town for a few nights. Okay, this is better than nothing. So, Alice helps me load up her little car with all my belongings that I have stored in her garage, and we begin heading up the mountains. Alice doesn't speak to me at all, and I can tell she is nervous because she hates driving in the snow. But this is her decision.

As we drive up the mountains, the snow is coming down heavier, and my India-conditioned body is freezing. I have neither snow boots nor a warm jacket, just a light fleece. I feel very anxious, and I know I am heading into a situation that will be very different than Amma's ashram. I pull out my Archana book and silently chant the thousand names of the Divine Mother. I am calling on Amma with all my heart to help me. As I chant, I feel myself surrendering this situation to Mother; I can do nothing. As I chant and feel my burden getting a little lighter, Alice's irritation becomes more apparent.

When we drive into the valley of Telluride, it dumps and blows snow. Alice drops me and all my life's belongings onto the front porch of Joe's house and leaves me with an awkward goodbye. I am left by myself. I leave my boxes stacked on the front porch, open the door to the house, and find no one is home. Joe told me he has two roommates, and I know a little about both. Walking into the house, I notice it is freezing; they must be trying to save on utilities. After I put my stuff in the garage, I find Joe's room and crawl under the covers on the bed, trying to get warm. Soon, I fall asleep.

Sometime later, I hear someone in the house, so I go out to greet them. It is the female roommate, Sid. She is a yoga teacher, and I brought her to see Amma once a few years ago in Santa Fe. She is surprised to see me in her house, so I explain that Joe is letting me stay in his room until I figure something out. I can tell that this has caught her off guard, but she smiles and tells me it is good to see me.

The next day, I see Sid again, and she is pretty unpleasant with me. She tells me she doesn't appreciate not knowing that I am staying here, and she tells me that I am being disrespectful of her space. Oh no. My shell of pretending to be "normal" starts to crack. I cannot go through this again. Sid tells me I should leave and find another place to live. She also tells me I should have it more together when I return from India, so I am not so dependent on others. She has no idea I have little choice in all this, that I am just trying to survive. I cannot explain myself to her; she would never understand what drives my life. I feel there is nowhere to turn; I have run out of options. I cannot pretend to be "normal and friendly" anymore. As the tears start to fall, I sense Sid getting more irritated with me, as if the sight of my tears is proof of my disrespect for her. I feel no disrespect towards her and understand where she comes from. But I simply cannot hold this phony act together anymore. My heart is breaking, and I feel my whole world collapse; I feel like God has abandoned me. I go and sit on the couch, and I ask Sid what she wants me to do. Gone is the act of being nice. Sid tells me I can stay one more night and leaves the room.

The next day, Joe calls me. He tells me he spoke with Sid, informing her I am staying in his room as his guest. I stay for a couple more days, then head outside town and put up a tent. Thank God the snow had stopped.

We all know what it is like to want a particular experience. We would rather feel better than worse, and we generally gravitate towards circumstances that make us feel good and secure and give us a feeling of well-being. This is a natural tendency of our body and nervous system, and this drive towards having a good experience runs in most people. People are trying to find the best experience or feeling and maintain it. Our society even supports this by telling us to feel positive and look happy by smiling and telling everyone all the good things happening in our lives. We want to maintain a positive image so that others will like us. We might not even want to talk about things when we don't feel good, feel like the world is gloomy, and feel our sense of worth slipping away. We become reluctant to share our challenges with others and will try to work things out independently rather than burden others with our fears. We want to appear strong and able rather than vulnerable in the eyes of our community. Even if it is false, a sense of strength gives us the illusion that we are still in control.

When we find spirituality, there might be hopes and promises of a better experience, with the spiritual experience being the ultimate one. Many people are drawn to spiritual practices to relieve their suffering, which is only natural. Spirituality is a great place to find techniques to help alleviate suffering. People start to feel more relaxed after meditation, and many go to retreats where the idea of meditating all day for many days sounds ideal. When we sit in the silence of presence, we can feel a great connectedness, which might feel like a burden lifted.

I see a strange tendency in folks interested in spirituality to think that we should eventually get to a place where nothing should ever bother us. The belief is that we should accept everything and always remain positive. These ideas can be very misleading when confused by feelings of contraction or insecurity. If we believe we should be stable and then encounter instability, we tend to judge the instability. To evolve as consciousness, we must look at our beliefs around our experiences. Given the right circumstances, we cannot know what internal experience will arise. Trying to control our internal experience according to our beliefs is just being phony; it is not real. If we do not take full responsibility for our feelings, we will miss the opportunity to dissolve the separate self. Instead, we will blame our feelings on our circumstances.

Simply put, we become victims, and life is just something that happens to us. We become powerless in life's grip of good days and bad, and the drive towards feeling "better" becomes the densest trance from which we can operate. If we encounter difficult emotions, we might even feel like victims of those emotions. We may start to identify with them. We might start thinking of ourselves as a sad person or an angry person. We can even put on a phony, happy face and think ourselves upbeat, calm, and positive. Getting in touch with what is currently relevant is crucial for our evolution.

Our minds are incredibly powerful in creating a sense of reality. If we believe we are an unhappy, miserable person, life will provide us with the right circumstances to support that belief. But if we are in denial of our true feelings, then life will continually give us those circumstances until we finally get in touch with those buried feelings. This is the trickiness of the mind's beliefs and their power. To think that you are your internal experience is akin to putting yourself in a prison cell. Why would you want to do that? To fully embody the Infinite, we must teach the brain that all feelings and emotions are normal and safe. We are not the emotions; we are what allows them.

Questioning any kind of self-identification or labeling invites openness. If we think we are sad, insecure, cool, or spiritually evolved, we must question the thought that says we are. Recognizing how we identify with our emotions is how we begin to recognize the separate self. We can recognize the patterns of our mind if we remain open enough to access clarity. We access clarity from Awareness. Acknowledging difficult feelings is a huge first step. What happens after the acknowledgment is crucial. If we have any beliefs about who and what kind of person we are, the next step may become problematic, as it was for me when I tried to appear "normal. "In those early years of my journey, I had no idea about emotional repression or bypassing. But Life gave me the circumstances I needed to break that pattern of trying to appear "normal."

Pure Awareness has no beliefs about what kind of person we should be. It only sees and allows. It has no hidden agendas. Allowing feelings, even intense ones, brings conscious awareness into the body. Allowing also signals to the brain that emotion is safe. By allowing all feelings, the brain can change its programs from the past into new information. When we allow feelings, we bring safety into the brain and dissolve the separate self's need for a positive identity. The challenge here is to be consistent with allowing because the false self will resist it repeatedly. Allowing is a skill to learn and practice. Allowing is infusing consciousness into the feeling, which negates wrongful identification as the emotion. We are not the emotion; we are what allows it.

There are no "bad" or wrong emotions, but if we tend to define ourselves (false selves) by our feelings, we will label them as good or bad, and unconscious resistance will ensue. We will automatically connect them to the circumstances in our lives, maybe even blaming our emotions on others. If we think others are causing our feelings, we will project a "story" onto them, perpetuating our fundamental separation. This continues the false self narrative, building and fortifying our prison walls.

None of this is fundamentally true, of course. Circumstances can trigger emotions, but all feelings originate within us. Life circumstances trigger them to come to the subconscious level. And that's where either resistance or allowing happens.

If we want to "feel better" by escaping our emotional identification, we then use techniques that promise freedom from emotions. Some methods may help us see the necessary patterns and tendencies of the false self. Still, if the drive towards a better experience remains while we deny the underlying emotions or latent tendencies, we will cover up the source of separation within us. The slippery mechanisms of emotional repression are cunning and hidden, and they're all designed to keep false identification within the mind-body complex safe.

We may secretly hope to become a better, more secure, enlightened person. We may hear spiritual teachings and convince ourselves that they will eventually save us from our present internal experience by giving us a better one. The silent promise of "it's going to get better someday" perpetuates the drive to feel better. The drive towards a better experience is ancient, a "wanting" that originates from the sense of lack or incompleteness within. If we believe—even subtly– that our internal experience is not the right experience, we will never have access to the depths of what is already here. To evolve the system, we need to bring awareness to the experience of NOW.

There is nothing wrong with wanting to have a better experience. If we have difficult programs from the past, perhaps caused by a challenging childhood or relationships, we want to heal those programs.

But if we deny them first, we are not allowing the Light of Awareness to alchemize them. We don't need to dig back into the past, as everything will arise at the right moment, but learning how to meet everything is essential. The healing part is in the allowing. When we begin to experience what the power of allowing is, from consciousness, we will want to bring it into our system more than we will want a better experience.

If we are looking for a better experience without meeting this one, we will miss out on a tremendous opportunity. And even if we do find a better experience, it will not last, and our undesirable emotions will still be there under the surface, ready to bother us at the slightest provocation. Sooner or later, we will realize that looking for a better experience isn't working out so well. It would be helpful to stop where you are and ask yourself: "What are you looking for? And why?"

This is a beneficial first question. It allows us to be honest about what we want. Your answer might originate from the false self, such as having a secure life with lots of friends and money. The important thing is to be honest here. Usually, if we get an answer like that, we at least have a place to start from—where we can begin to unravel the false drive for security, which can lead to more profound questions. If we're honest, a revealing space can open within our consciousness. If we tell ourselves we want enlightenment when we really want a better experience, we won't do so well with inquiry. If we are honest with our inquiry, we are opening as consciousness and accessing more profound intelligence.

We are often unaware of the unconscious drives that may control us, so asking simple questions can open us up and access more clarity. The intelligence within is waiting to be activated, and we can access it by asking simple questions. We can begin to access our most authentic and reliable Divine connection within. Asking questions is the way to open a doorway and establish a deep and lasting relationship with ourselves. The entire Universe is waiting for us to get curious, and if we can remain open and objective and not controlled by our desire for a better experience, a deep internal intelligence can respond. Even if we can be honest about our desire for a better moment, we can still access this illuminating inner clarity–if we stay open. The most important thing is that we access authenticity. It's about being real.

How we use questions is very important. This is not another technique to get us out of our difficult emotions. Many folks will adopt self-inquiry as an attempt to avoid themselves. They may think they don't need to work on themselves if their true essence is already present. So, being transparent about our intentions is vital. Inquiry is not a way out of ourselves but a way to open our consciousness to see clearly. Clarity is the golden ticket. We are conscious Awareness, so asking questions to access and strengthen this Awareness can be highly beneficial. Awareness is like an essential muscle; the more we use it, the stronger and more effective it becomes. It's our superpower to access and embody the Infinite.

Many people miss what they feel right now; the programs that run them are set on automatic, and since they miss them, they miss the opportunity to allow them. We must see stuff to change stuff. The stuff consists of programs from the past. We must get to know it inside and out. If we don't, we will remain under its influence, which is not freedom. If we are unconsciously driven towards feeling better or more expansive, we miss seeing the source of separation within.

If we ask ourselves a question, we can open a doorway, accessing a new perspective. A very effective question is, "What am I feeling right now? "And then, 'Can I allow myself to feel this?" I use a simple prompt and simply declare, "Allow." In the moment of allowing, we align ourselves with the Consciousness of allowing. It is free of agenda and has a massive message of safety for the mind-body complex, enabling it to relax into the present moment. This relaxing dissolves the unconscious drives of separation; it dismantles it.

When we ask these questions, we are not trying to get in touch with a feeling so that it goes away; we are accessing the field of consciousness that allows the feeling. This question uses our feelings to awaken the dynamics of inner Awareness. Consciousness naturally responds to the question simply because it *already* allows the feeling. The question accesses consciousness so that it can be conscious of itself. In doing so, our identification with the feeling shifts. Our feelings or emotions become objective and no longer "personal." We no longer feel that our feelings are "ours." When we no longer personalize an emotion by making it "mine," it can be pure and free. All the energy of trying to manage an emotion can also be freed up. It takes a lot of energy to manage our feelings, so when bound energy is released, it returns to the conscious life force from which it came.

The Consciousness within our being has a great capacity to know itself through feeling. It recognizes itself within the nervous system through feeling. When you ask yourself, "Can I allow this experience?" you might notice an immediate dropping into yourself, and the old impulse of wanting the feeling to go away weakens–it may even dissolve altogether. This is when you know you are in the realm of pure feeling. This is when Consciousness is having the experience, not the separate self. The old drive to have a better moment simply can't sustain itself in this realm. The separate self is absent since it *is* the drive for a better moment. We can now perceive, through the perception of Conscious Awareness, our True Self. Our experience is pure. We aren't attempting to control it because consciousness does not try to control anything. We experience our deepest, most intense feelings through the lens of consciousness. This new perspective is our natural home; it is what we are. Consciousness becomes conscious of itself through our feelings and emotions. It is so simple. No matter the feeling or intensity of emotion, the opportunity is always within us.

When we ask questions that awaken consciousness, old tendencies that have been with us our entire life can begin to surface. We never even knew they were there. The more emotions and feelings are allowed, the more they get freed up. Our filters (the separate self) that have always managed our experience begin to fall away, maybe even to the point where we lose all ability to manage all feelings. There might be a period in our process where all our unconscious emotions come rushing to the surface, which may be intense. We might feel totally out of control at times. See if there is resistance to it and where that might come from. The dissolving of the separate self triggers the sense of the loss of control.

We might use inquiry with every honest intention to awaken consciousness, yet there can still be a belief that "we know how" to be with our feelings. This belief can prevent us from accessing conscious awareness, keeping us from having false self-identity. We unconsciously maintain the separate self's belief that it "knows." If the separate self thinks it knows how to be with something, we can get stuck–maybe for a long time. We might develop a certain "way" to be with an emotion, which can become rigid and stagnant. It doesn't access that which allows. It just becomes another coping strategy that the controller hides behind. I have seen many people get stuck in their type of processing because they believe they know how to get through their emotions, but the feelings keep coming, and they haven't accessed that which allows. The separate self's identification is still within the emotions, and as a result, the emotional body may take on a kind of edginess. The emotional body is not evolving; it is not being nourished through safety by being wholly allowed. If we think "we know how" to be with our experience, but truthfully, we just want to get through it so the "bad" feelings will go away, we might not be able to access the pure consciousness that allows. "Do I know how to be with these feelings?" The question opens and exposes any energy within us that is trying to control.

We are beginning to expose programs that still *believe* in the need to control. This is a crucial first step in healing our mind-body and accessing pure Awareness. We wake ourselves from the trance of identity within emotions by asking honest questions. This spiritual maturity is awakening and opening to our true nature, an open field of objectivity, utterly free of control. This also means we do not avoid anything, which is another form of control. The more we evolve as consciousness, the easier it is to recognize control. Pure consciousness meets everything profoundly and objectively.

The paradox about letting go of control is that we begin to see how powerful we are in shifting our relationship with experience. Once we can access this vast Field of Awareness, we can learn to master our interpretations of life experiences. We can learn to give the brain new information so that it doesn't stay stuck in the rigid patterns of the past. We can enhance the brain's capacity to choose from different responses rather than the old predictive reactions. This is when things get fun- learning to master results from allowing and relinquishing false control.

Asking questions with the right attitude opens the door to deep intelligence within. If we can keep the door open, we will experience life with an ever-increasing intimacy, a newness we have never known.

When we genuinely welcome this moment, without any control, it is a brand-new moment–it has never happened before. It is fresh because the separate self is not relating to it from what it thinks it knows. Anything is possible in the absence of control. Life flows through us, inviting us to participate more intuitively rather than just trying to make something happen. We have access to fresh, dynamic energy, the same intelligent energy that blooms flowers and makes the sun rise. We can sense in our being that we are right where we need to be and are completely aligned with this moment in absolute coopera-tion. This is the Divine intelligence awakening within; it is the heart's intelligence. We can feel a deep, silent presence within our beings and our bodies—a presence that knows how to evolve to its fullest poten-tial. This potential is our Divine blueprint as creative energy. This is what we are here for: to become a vehicle for this energy. And the Field of consciousness knows just how to do this.

6.

The Nervous System and Sri Yantra

Once you learn the art of relaxation,
everything happens spontaneously and effortlessly.

~Sri Mata Amritanandamayi Devi

2003. It is my last year in India; I know this deeply and intuitively. I try to spend as much time as possible in Amma's presence, and she rewards me with lots of long, deep gazes, even when thousands of people are around. She does this continuously throughout the day, every day. I sit still and open as I feel her pouring into me.

I am sitting in front of the stage as Amma gives Darshan. We are in the Kali temple, and the Kali Murti (statue) is right behind Amma. About thirty Westerners are sitting on the floor before Amma, and we can see her very well. A male disciple is standing beside Amma, showing her some plans. They look like blueprints of a building. Amma has someone in her lap. She looks over these plans, and the disciple explains them to her. Suddenly, Amma turns to look at me as she talks to the disciple beside her. She gestures with her hands, making specific angular shapes like describing a particular design. She keeps looking at me while she is doing this. As Amma makes these plans with her hands, she does so with great conviction, as if she knows this is how it needs to be. Occasionally, she releases the person in her lap, and a new one steps in for their Darshan, but she never takes her eyes off me as she continues to talk to the disciple about the design.

Amma is telling me that there is a plan. She tells me that a design is already in place, and all I need to do is let it unfold. It is one of the most precise transmissions I have ever received from her. I feel my being responding in wonder; I am continually amazed at how Amma shares herself with her disciples. Amma has just awakened a design that is in me, and this design will manifest when the time is right.

Our central nervous system is marvelous and complex and has a tremendous capacity to evolve. It is a vast wiring of circuits and pathways that, through a shift of perception, can alter how we interpret Life. The brain is also part of this extensive network, signaling the mind-body complex on how to respond to the information it receives. The rest of the mind-body physiology, its cells, muscles, blood, etc., are directly linked to the impulses within our nervous system and will be affected as the system opens up.

We stay stuck when we operate from the old way of seeing things without ever questioning what we are feeling, what we believe, or how we interpret our thought processes. We can work through many emotional patterns, but without a sincere inquiry into how we (our mind) interpret emotions, thoughts, and the world, it will be much more difficult for any shift within our consciousness. A change of perception is a rewiring of our nervous system when our brain, body, and mind perceive and experience Life in a completely new way. This is where the core of evolution lies.

Have you ever firmly believed a story, and then something cracked in your consciousness, such as someone telling you that what you thought wasn't what happened, and afterward, you wondered how you could have believed your original perception? Your capacity to believe the old story isn't there anymore. This is a shift in perception, and it can feel incredibly liberating when it happens. This is because an old hard-wired neural network within the nervous system has been freed up. It's been given new information that signals a new pathway to be created. It's almost as if a light gets turned on inside, and you feel more spacious, whereas the old story felt fixed and rigid.

When we are open, the pathways of our nervous system can, in an organic way, discover new ways of interpreting Life, freeing us from old, fixed perceptions. This is where the most profound transformations come from, and when we have significant shifts out of the separate self, these pathways can open and operate more efficiently. Our perception of life becomes clearer and aligns with the rest of life with greater resilience. Our personal interpretations of Life begin to fade so that what we perceive has nothing to do with "us." We are moved by life and can now experience this more objectively, rather than from a "me, or a center." Our perceptions can be viewed *from* Life, which is completely impersonal, yet includes it.

The nervous system is the divine blueprint we all carry within the body. It is the limbs and extension of the unfathomable organ called the brain. We are said to use only a fraction of our brain's capacity, but we can use so much more. Maybe this is where that deep intuitive sense—that we are capable of so much more—is coming from. Is the brain the seat of intuitive knowing? Is the Divine consciousness within the brain sending out intuitive messages that urge us on our evolutionary journey?

On a basic level, the brain's job is to keep the mind-body safe. The brain takes in tons of information, especially when we are kids, just for this purpose. All information is stored in the neural networks, deep in the unconscious. And because it is unconscious, we are unaware of most of this information. The evolutionary process is to open and reveal this information to see if it is obsolete. If this information is still being stored unconsciously while being obsolete, our mind-body complex is operating on an outdated system. This outdated system is not keeping us safe; it is keeping us imprisoned. We can never feel free when we are living within an obsolete system.

We are such a profound mystery that asks for exploration, and the nervous system is the doorway to that exploration.

When we feel a particular feeling, an "experience," we feel it in our nervous system. If we separate ourselves from thinking and experience, it becomes a pure feeling. It is a felt experience or a pure experience. The nervous system feels it, which can feel subtle or intense and everything in between. A pure experience is one where we are acutely aware of the experience through feeling and allowing it.

We want to feel it objectively, so we do not identify with it. There is no agenda to get through; it is allowed most purely. Even getting to this degree of allowing is part of evolution, and I am amazed at how the capacity to have a pure experience evolves. The nervous system is discovering its capacity to open to pure experience and recognizing that pure experience is not harmful to its system. Through this, the brain takes in the information that the experience is safe. The brain begins to change the neural networks associated with the experience. It starts firing and wiring new information. The nervous system begins recognizing its natural function within the experience: opening and feeling without any associated identification or danger. It feels safe and free of any previous rigidity.

The nervous system keeps us from harm. It recognizes when we put our finger in the fire; the brain sends the signal to pull it out because it hurts. We get the message to eat and get warm when we are cold and hungry. So, generally, the nervous system is accustomed to keeping us safe and free from harm. But if programmed only for that purpose, it will interpret any experience as good or bad, harmful or helpful. This is a minimal function for such a fantastic system.

When we feel and then identify with an intense, uncomfortable experience, our nervous system interprets it as wrong or harmful. The identity makes it about "me." The mind takes that interpretation and programs itself not to want a "bad" experience. The identified mind thinks of itself as a person that needs to be happy, so it only wants happy, feel-good experiences. What happens then is an automatic mechanism kicks in; it's the mechanism to either resist through a contraction or to repress or dismiss the experience as being valid (spiritual bypassing falls into this category) or even to default to another feeling that the brain thinks is safer. This happens automatically without conscious awareness, all because of the unconscious identification with a separate self.

When that first essential shift out of the separate self occurs, many filters to "keep out the bad" disappear. When the filters are gone, the nervous system can experience and feel everything in a pure way. I have mentioned that a lot of energy can be released after a shift in consciousness. I have seen people physically shaking from loads of energy being freed up within their nervous system. Some are laughing and crying simultaneously as the filters come down, and with it, part of the separate self that made up those filters. This is one of the ways that the separate self begins to dissolve. Now, we are in the realm of pure feeling, and it's the best place we can be for the nervous system.

The nervous system's capacity to open to pure feelings is tremendous. It is a system of pure sensing and intuiting. It can also inform us if we are operating from illusion, through contraction, or aligned with the natural flow of life. Evolution is about getting to know in a feeling and sensing our most profound connection to the whole of existence, both seen and unseen. To feel connected in this way will give us great courage to continue, which is what we want. We want to stay inspired. When this connection becomes strong and resilient, it is allowed, and we can begin to relax in a way we have never experienced before. Amma says true enlightenment is "The art of relaxation." We might call this faith, but it is essentially the nervous system feeling its absolute connection with the source of all creation. It feels like a vessel for this source and feels cared for through intimacy with source consciousness. The mind-body begins to be informed in a new way, not through the old programs from the past, but through the Totality of the present.

This is not a mere concept to put in your pocket but to discover within yourself. If we take this exploration of ourselves seriously, Grace can show us exactly why we have this design within us. The human nervous system is designed to adapt, change, and evolve. If it is influenced by something other than the old paradigm of the separate self, it can evolve to go beyond that paradigm. As we refine our skills of pure allowing, we allow the Infinite Totality into the system. And when you sense that this is happening to you, you learn how to get out of the way. Pure allowing can then evolve into Full Access. The Totality knows how to do this—it knows just what to do to develop the mind-body complex to make it a fit vessel for itself, an instrument for the Divine.

The nervous system is designed to be a vessel for the Infinite field of consciousness. When your nervous system begins to be informed by this Field, it will be the ultimate message of safety for your brain. The brain starts recognizing that it doesn't need to interpret its environment non-stop for signs of danger because the Field is taking care of everything. Of course, this takes time, focused intention, and devotion to the Field. But this is the spiritual journey, right?

In India's ancient Vedic philosophical system, there is a symbol called the Sri Yantra. It consists of nine triangles going out from the center in opposite directions. Within the very center of the Yantra is a tiny black dot or portal. This Yantra in the Vedic system represents the world of form or the Divine Mother. It is also thought to be a map from material existence to enlightenment.

We exist in the world of form. Our emotions, thoughts, and belief patterns are all forms, as are the denser, more apparent forms around us in the physical world. The relative world we experience around us is a limited manifestation within three dimensions. When we identify ourselves with the world of form, we identify our entire existence within material existence.

When we gaze at the Sri Yantra, we see an ever-expanding field of multidimensional reality. There are many interpretations of the Sri Yantra, but if we use our sensing system, the patterns can take us beyond definition. It is a symbol of the great Mystery, and if we remain open to this mystery in our daily lives, something can shift within our consciousness, opening the nervous system.

When the nervous system senses within itself a greater capacity than the one it is experiencing, it senses that there is more than the three-dimensional reality it perceives. The Sri Yantra design within the nervous system activates that knowing or sensing, inspiring the nervous system to keep opening. It allows the nervous system to sense its ever-expanding field within itself, just like the Sri Yantra. The Sri Yantra invites us into the center, the Bindu, the tiny portal with the potential for all manifestation. The Bindu is pure nothingness, empty of all form.

When we sense through the nervous system, we may intuit an intelligence that invites us into the depths of this moment. We are opening to this pristine moment through our nervous system while leaving behind all previously believed forms. This moment is the

Bindu of the Sri Yantra, and it is *here* that we may enter the greater mystery as we leave the known behind.

The more we associate with the Bindu or pristine moment, the more we offer ourselves to the Unknown or great mystery. This association affects our nervous system profoundly, and the density of the separate self slowly begins to fade. It's another alchemical experience that the mind cannot explain. It can only be traveled through, again and again. It is this repetition that changes the brain's understanding of Life. This is how neuroscience creates change: through constant repetition. This is why spiritual practices are so important. Amma says meditation, which goes into the Bindu, is like gold.

All spiritual experiences are merely to keep the nervous system inspired, to give it a taste of its true capacity so that it may open beyond its previous perceptions. Spiritual experiences do not mean the self is more advanced; they have nothing to do with advancement. They are gifts, but they can stop the evolutionary process if they are grabbed onto. Westerners love an out-of-the-box experience, so much of the Western spiritual world is bent on getting a great experience. This is not what true spirituality is about, yet grabbing will happen because of the separate self's unconscious feelings of lack and separation. And while I enjoy a thrilling experience as much as anyone, I am not looking for one. They happen and are finished, just like any other experience. When an experience happens, it is allowed with full access to the nervous system. The incredible experiences that may happen from that inspire and inform the system on how to open even more.

A fantastic spiritual experience does not stop the "unpleasant" experiences either. I have had countless mind-blowing experiences, but I also had the wisdom to keep going, for they were merely signposts along the road. I needed those inspiring experiences then because I also had many difficult emotional patterns that needed healing. Those early days were very challenging for me, and it often felt like the emotional intensity wouldn't ever end. The peak experiences inspired me; they helped relax the nervous system so it wouldn't be so tweaked. They also showed me that the openings from spiritual experiences have their place in the purification process. I have seen patterns of "clearings," where a massive spiritual experience would happen, and right after, a deep, emotional purge would come up. The experiences have also changed from fantastic to more informative with downloaded information. When we experience how the nervous system evolves into a receptacle for information from the Field, we learn how to stay completely out of the way and experience the wonder of the Great Mystery.

There can be many obstacles or tests along the way. We must remain clear about what we are here for and what this process is about. When we see that we do not know with our minds where we are headed, we can stay open and humble. This is why we have the ancient texts of Vedanta, which show us how to live and why we have a human birth.

When the nervous system starts to open, we sense that anything is possible. We are staying open to the intelligence of the design within us. We might discover we have gifts, such as healing or psychic abilities. If we stay mindful, we will not be in danger of the separate self "owning" these gifts. Any "owning" will keep us on the three-dimensional side of reality. The evolutionary process has a safety valve within its design. The false self can't enter the Bindu within the Divine Blueprint; the separate self must be dissolved before we can access our infinite potential. The separate self cannot go beyond this three-dimensional reality, which is its realm. We cannot have personal agendas if we want to embody a new paradigm or have access to a multi-dimensional existence. This keeps the evolutionary process very pure and of the highest integrity.

When we have a pure emotional experience within the nervous system, it flushes the old system. Maybe you have felt this after allowing an intense emotion to move through you. We feel cleaned out and almost new afterward, like fresh and reborn. You may have noticed how everything in life takes on a new clarity, and life shimmers and sparkles all around you. The sky is a deeper blue, and the birdsong is the most fantastic sound ever; Life seems miraculous. This is because you see Life through new eyes, now governed by an updated nervous system. The nervous system is giving you this new vision. If we can keep nurturing any opening by not going back and clinging to our old perceptions, our vision will continue to evolve. But of course, we will-that is the nature of the old paradigm; it has a strong pull back into familiarity. But if we can keep revisiting the Unknown through our practice and keep allowing emotions, the nervous system will begin to open so much that the old familiar cannot pull us back anymore. When our vision evolves through the nervous system, the relative world stops being so darn real. We now know that things are not just as they appear. The nervous system informs our vision because it has begun to sense what is true. It senses its function as a vessel for the vast field of consciousness, the reality within everything, seen and unseen.

When the nervous system knows its evolved function, the programs of the separate self begin to be replaced by a new occupant. This new occupant is the Universal Self or Eternal Being. It is a presence entirely absent of any identity; it is empty, yet completely conscious. The Universal Self is not a new identity but an absence of identity. Only the separate self would create a new identity. This is why ancient texts repeatedly teach us that we must first remove the ignorance of the separate self.

The separate self comprises beliefs, opinions, memories, and identity. The spiritual ego is a separate self that thinks it knows. It is still an identity. This is a very easy trap to fall into, and it is something that we all go through. But with a competent guide, we can be assured that false identities can't delude us long. The guide will lovingly (or not) show us how miserable a spiritual ego can be. When we think we know something, we are not in the Bindu but back in the 3-D reality of the separate self. And this takes a lot of energy to maintain. The belief that "we know" begins to drain the nervous system of life force, and we begin to stagnate and dry up.

Whereas the Universal Self is an effortless knowing; it knows itself. It is *Purnam*, or completeness. It is the Bindu.

When the nervous system is freed from false identity, it lights up. This is the activation of the Divine Blueprint within each of us or our unborn potential. Amma says that when she sees us, she sees our Divine Blueprint or the Perfect Jewel. She sees the potential within us, and, as a Master, she begins to cut away our illusions to bring out the brilliance of that jewel. She is cutting away all the beliefs and personal agendas out of the system. When we experience this cutting away or dissolution over some time, it can feel like a part of us is dying. It is the dying of the separate self.

The lighting up of the Divine Blueprint, the evolved nervous system, is the birth of a new human being. It is the birth of what the Buddhists call the Light Body or the Rainbow Body. This body does not conform to the old definitions that we gave our biological systems. This new organism is beyond limitation, although it has no self to own it. The pure light of consciousness, or Universal Self, is living in this body. It is a tool in the hands of the Totality. There are many stories about the Light Body, monks taking their bodies with them when they die, or sages simultaneously being in more than one place. Many devotees have experienced this with Amma, as I have. Did not Jesus tell us, when we were amazed by His feats, that there were many more things we would do? We must consider these things as possible and keep our minds open. They are not miracles; they are a product of a great miracle—the evolution of the nervous system within you.

7.

Grief and Love in the Bathtub

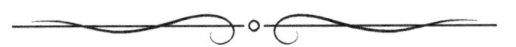

Grief can be the garden of compassion.
If you keep your heart open through everything,
your pain can become your greatest ally in your life's search
for love and wisdom.

~RUMI

1986. It's the day of my 28ᵗʰ birthday, and it's a beautiful spring day in Lake Tahoe, California. I look out my window at the Truckee River at the edge of my yard and realize something has changed overnight. It's my birthday, and I am not the person I was yesterday. I've lived a fun-filled life with many friends and parties, but I no longer want that life. I am not finding any satisfaction in that life.

For much of my youth, it has felt as if I was trying to get to something, trying to break through some invisible barrier into a depth that I can sense is here. I have always been aware of an unseen presence around me, and I have always known there was much more than what we see in everyday life. When I was a child, I would talk to the "little people" who were present, and I felt very alone and misunderstood by adults. So, as a young adult, I started to party to ease the constant discomfort that I experienced. Afterward, I would always have to come back to my insecure and sensitive self. So today, I feel done with this dead-end cycle of misery. I feel entirely different today, and I don't know what it is, but I know I must find out.

So, I go outside into the warm sunshine and walk down to the river. I sit down by the bank and close my eyes. It's as if the entire universe is waiting for this moment because I immediately enter a deeply absorbed state of meditation. It feels like a powerful force is pushing me to stay seated, so I couldn't move if I wanted to. This deep state of meditation feels natural to me, and I can sense that I already know how to do this, maybe from another time. Suddenly, my awareness/self is lifting out of my body, which also feels effortless. I am amazed by this tremendous experience as I leave my body on the riverside below. Now, my consciousness expands beyond anything I have ever known. I am BIG! I am beyond any definition. I can't even begin to explore this new experience when WHAM! Suddenly, a great force shoves me back down HARD. It's like the hand of God has come and pushed me back into my body. I am so startled I open my eyes. What the? What was that?

Whatever that force was, I feel like I know it, as if I have an intimate relationship with it. It feels like a parent or a "bigger" being. The part of me that wanted to leave the body was the real me, and the body without that part of me is nothing at all. I am not just this birthday girl sitting on the riverbank; yet I have no clue what I am. My life has changed, and now I want to do it again! I want to know what that force was that shoved me back into my body! I want to know how I learned to do that floating out-of-body thing.

I begin meditating at least once daily, which is extremely enjoyable and inspiring. My soul tries to leave the body a few more times, but the hand of God always comes and shoves me back in with such force that I'm beginning to understand that I am not to do that anymore. I am meant to stay in my body this time around.

I am now on a super-high spiritual honeymoon. I am still relatively young and have started to exercise regularly and eat much better. I have lots of energy and feel incredibly inspired by my new spiritual awareness. I begin taking trips into the wilderness of the Sierra Nevada Mountains by myself, sometimes for many days. I like being alone in nature, where I can feel the unseen presence more intimately. This connection with presence feels highly precious to me, and I only want to deepen it, so I find myself doing ceremonies in the Native American style, calling on the four directions and all the subtle beings to aid me in my search. I don't know how I know how to do this, but it feels perfect when I do it. When I pray with all my heart to this vast presence, I can feel the entire mystery respond. This is what I was looking for when I did drugs, and now I know it was in me the whole time. I begin to feel empowered and blessed by this recognition.

I begin to travel all over the Southwest, searching out the sacred sites of the ancient kingdoms. I enter the Great Kivas and circles and call upon all the powers of the unseen mystery. This newfound life fills me with so much inspiration and happiness that I am soaring. I know the source of creation, and my being radiates from this awareness. My spiritual honeymoon lasts for about two years, and then things begin to change.

I am traveling through northern Arizona when a car pulls out of nowhere and smashes into the side of my truck. It is terribly inconvenient, as I must put it in the shop for three weeks. So, the Toyota dealer in Flagstaff gives me this little tin-can car to drive, and I head down Oak Creek Canyon to Sedona.

Sedona, Arizona, in the mid-80s, is a sweet little town. It has just become incorporated as a town, and even though I am forced to hang out here while my truck is repaired, I feel blessed by it all. I have started to meet people and spend my days hiking around the sacred red rocks. It is so stunningly beautiful. I keep pinching myself to see if I am here. The natural beauty of the red rocks and the powerful earth energy that radiates from the place has me spellbound. And the more friends I make here, the more I know I want to stay. I want to live in Sedona. I soon met Monica, who rents me a room in her house. I now live in Sedona!

Shortly after I move into my new house, I begin to feel very emotional, and I don't know why. I am getting irritated easily, and after such a spiritual high, this new emotional intensity concerns me. Sometimes, I feel like I am losing control as these grippy emotions become more consistent.

I am driving the little tin can down the road, and a panic grips me. The car in front of me is going slow, so I yell at it to pull over; I rage at it with my whole being. And the car pulls right over, and I drive by. When I get home, I go into the living room and totally lose it. The room has no furniture, so I sit on the floor and lean against the wall. I feel a big dark hole open before me and am freaked out.

My world goes black—a void. I am standing on a cliff, wracked with grief. Native American. My entire family has been slaughtered. I jump.

When I return to the present, I am shaken to my core. This is way too much for me. But the universe comes to my rescue, giving me everything I need. I immediately talk to Monica, my landlady. The universe has dropped me right into Monica's lap, who happens to be an internationally known psychic. Monica tells me that I have come to Sedona to clear up a past lifetime and will soon meet someone who will help me.

Several days later, I am participating in a Native American ceremony called a "Yuwipi." A well-known Lakota medicine man is leading it, and it is one of the most remarkable events I have ever seen. Spirits are flying, and I hear their voices singing behind me as the medicine man sings the sacred songs.

A few days later, the medicine man calls me and invites me to his family's house for dinner! I will spend much time with this family over the next two years. We travel all over Arizona doing ceremonies for tribes losing their land. I sleep in hogans on the dirt floor with goats and sheep. I make new friends I relate to as if I have known them. This medicine man is the person who has come into my life to help me clear out my troubled past life. My relationship with the Lakota people becomes highly intense at times as I revisit this past life and all the pain associated with it. Even though I love the ceremonies, prayers, and honoring of the Great Spirit, I do not feel safe. I am a 29-year-old white woman, and I have become increasingly more aware of the complicated and painful karma between the Lakota and the white people. Yet Love is more potent, and over time, through powerful traditional ceremonies, I feel the karmic bond start to loosen.

My health is starting to decline. After being so fit and healthy, I find it quite challenging not to feel well. I have had some digestive issues flare up, so I began to visit health practitioners for help. I go to naturopaths, acupuncturists, and doctors, and soon, I will spend all my savings on various health and cleansing regimes. And every day, I only feel more exhausted. I became too sick to work, and because I am running out of money, I am stressed out, too. Nothing I do helps this mystery disease, and I am getting weaker; it gets to the point where I can no longer get out of bed. I can no longer keep up a conversation because I can't understand what is being said. I can't read books either because I don't know what I am reading, and I have always been an avid reader. When I go see a doctor, I break down in tears, and the doctor looks at me like I am a total basket case. I feel so desperately lost; I feel like I am sinking into a deep, dark hole.

I take my little savings and move into my own apartment. I need to be alone in my darkness. My diet becomes vegetable juices and spirulina because I cannot digest anything else, and it only makes me sicker if I do eat. I no longer go to any health care practitioners. My time with the medicine man has come to an end as I no longer feel drawn to that path; it seems that what needed to be done with the Native Americans is now complete. I find myself turning inside myself. I begin to pray a lot and call to God. I need God; I need help. But even more than that, I feel a longing for communion with God; I want God to take me away. The grief and pain that I felt earlier as an unfamiliar emotion is now deepening into a much purer longing for God, for Truth. When I pray, I declare, "I want to come home." I say this over and over every day. I know I am very sick, and my life is falling apart, but something is emerging from this deep grief. I sense that grief is a doorway into something new.

I take long baths every night, and when I am in the bathtub, the grief opens. As soon as I relax, the grief appears like an old friend. I pray to God while feeling intense grief in my heart and my body, and the grief begins to open in my body, just like a lotus flower. The grief is starting to reveal that this grief has never been allowed to have a voice. So, now I allow the grief to have a voice. The prayers emerging from my heart have profound wisdom to them. The words tell the truth about where the grief comes from. Grief is saying that I want God; I want to go home. I have been away for so long that I have lost the connection with the most precious part of myself. I need to find that essential part of myself again because the pain of losing it is just too unbearable. Deep grief is leading me back to myself, back to the part of myself that I cherish above all else. The grief is allowing me to reconnect with the most essential part of my being and to fall in Love again.

As grief is allowed to deepen and be pure, a new presence comes to me- a powerful presence of Love and Compassion. It feels like the blessed Mother Mary, only different. She feels like the Mother of all, holding me close. She comes to me every day, and she knows everything about me. She has come to tell me that I am not alone, that I have her. She tells me she will never leave me and that I am her child. I have never experienced anything so wondrous in my whole life. I feel supported and loved, and I know I will never be alone again. My heart begins to open to Her, and all I can think about is Her holding me and the feelings it evokes in me, feelings of a Love so sacred, Divine, and precious. My prayers take on a new beginning, and the pain in my heart becomes a longing for Her. I don't want to come home so much anymore. I want Her.

When I experienced such profound grief each night in the bathtub (and other times as well), I prayed for help. I felt so lost that I didn't know where to turn. I was as helpless as a newborn baby, and so I cried for help. When I completely surrendered into total vulnerability, it was then that a new presence came to me—the presence of the Divine Mother herself. She would come and hold me as I wept. I no longer felt alone and frightened when I felt her arms around me. It was the presence of Mother that birthed a new relationship with the Divine within my consciousness. The presence of the Divine Mother felt so incredibly beautiful and powerful that She became the new focus of all my longing. My heart longed to know the Divine Mother intensely, which was the beginning of my devotional path. It was also the beginning of the healing of my body, as all that repressed grief was allowed to express itself.

Within a year, I was out of bed and backpacking in the wilderness, feeling the presence of the Divine Mother everywhere. I would have occasional lapses of weakness, and I still have some of those old digestive issues, but I was never sick like that again.

Every night, I would pray to Mother to come to me, and I was rewarded by experiencing the most intimate connection in my heart. My heart longed for union with the Divine Mother, so I became her child. When I met Amma several years later, my heart was like ripe fruit made sweet by my longing for the Divine Mother. Amma saw this in me and made me her own. And within a short time, I realized that Amma was the same Mother that had come to me in my deep state of grief. It was She who was the same Mother that I longed for in my prayers. My devotion shifted from focusing on the formless to pure guru Bhakti, the most critical step in my spiritual journey.

This relationship has evolved and matured profoundly over the years. Amma has been holding me close ever since.

Using emotion, such as grief as a vehicle to the Divine, awakens the Divine intelligence within. The Divine within us knows how to open the heart, and emotions are a powerful way to access these deep, latent qualities of devotion within us. Allowing the power of emotion to propel us towards clarity and begin to dissolve unconscious ideas and beliefs is one of the purest ways to open to this great mystery. The intelligence within the Heart clears the cobwebs of muddled intellectual understandings and gathers all that energy to focus on the Divine. Getting to a place where we are so out of the way can be difficult if we rely on our intellectual understanding, but the energy of the Heart knows the way.

Divine intelligence within the Heart uses whatever the human being is experiencing to awaken. This isn't a process of becoming better or more "pure," but rather authentic and open. Being real activates consciousness. We are not conscious if we attempt to be something we are not.

Our emotions can be a potent energy that draws the Divine to us, activating our awareness of the Divine connection. The more we can learn to harness the energy behind emotions and offer it to the Divine through our focus, the stronger that connection can be. And through this connection, those emotions become purified and stabilized.

If we don't pollute our emotions with stories and beliefs, while wanting them to go away, they can open the heart to a wondrous love affair. It is a love affair of the highest order. If we aren't blaming our emotions on life, we can access a deep intelligence that is within them. This happened to me in the bathtub: grief finally found its voice. Strong emotions get our attention, and they have tremendous energy within them. We need something to get our attention in this dense dream world. If we allow these emotions to have a voice, we can discover what is ready to awaken within us.

Don't fear strong emotion; don't fear any intensity. Ask them if they need to say something, and then learn to listen. What are these deep feelings inside us? Perhaps they are only energies that are also looking for liberation.

Only the mind can decide if something is good or bad. Only the mind divides and fears intensity. By allowing it all, we are beginning to disarm the tendencies toward division that reside within us so that what is never divided can reveal itself.

8.

Om Parasaktyai Namah

(Salutations to She who is the Original,
Supreme Power)

The Mother of the Universe is here now, closer than you can imagine. The Divine Mother of all creation is present within all experience–She is the experience. Shakti is alive within all forms, as She is the substratum of all forms. To know the Mother and to fall deeply in Love with Her is to know yourself and fall deeply in Love with the essence of your true Self.

When we have a pure relationship with the Divine Mother, we are not looking for anything from Her; instead, we give our entire experience to Her. Only through the pure unconditional Love of the Universal Mother are we able to experience that every part of our human selves is already being allowed.

It is a challenge for me to write about the Divine Mother because of the intense intimacy that I have experienced with Her over the last few decades. Having a relationship with the Divine Mother isn't something the mind can ever comprehend, so it is not something you can imagine. And if it is not something the mind can understand, it is also not something to evaluate and intellectualize. For me, the relationship with the Supreme Shakti is the most precious experience I have, and it is the ONLY relationship in my life, as all relationships are a relationship with Her. She is everything to me; She is the reason I live. She is also Life's pulse that inspired me to write this book.

When I found myself comforted by the presence of the Divine Mother in the bathtub, my life started to change. Mother's presence opened a doorway I fell through, and an indescribable journey of Love and deep longing commenced. When Mother came to me in the bathtub, I knew it to be a gift, a grace. Her presence was like nothing I had ever experienced before, and even though I first knew Her to be a soothing comfort in my darkest time, I also sensed that She was so much more than just a presence. I sensed that She was the most incredible power that had borne the entire creation and that everything and everyone was Hers.

When my awareness of the Divine Mother began, I wanted her and nothing else. I would get up early every morning and pray to Her, and my longing for Her grew more intense each day. I had no idea why this longing consumed me, nor did I care. After the deep dark hole of illness, this Divine presence shone like a bright sun on my hopeless self. I started to lose interest in any outer life, even though I had enjoyed meeting many spiritually minded folks in Sedona. I didn't feel like I had room for anyone other than Her, so I stopped seeing anyone romantically. Mother was inside my heart as a strong feeling, and the more I longed for Her, the more She pulled me deeper inside. I was departing the world as I knew it and entering Her domain, the heart's domain.

Shakti is the power behind all forms. She is the substance of form and the intelligence that creates all form. We are Her creation, Her children. Shakti is not only our bodies but also our emotions, thoughts, and every belief and illusion. She is the grand illusion of Maya. She is everything we think of ourselves to be and everything we do not know ourselves to be. She is also the Divine Blueprint within all of creation, the pure potential we all carry.

When Mother came to me, and I felt my being respond to Her, I sensed that She wanted me even more than I ever wanted Her. The experience since that first day has been the same: Mother wants us—she wants every bit of us. She came to me because she created the circumstances that made me need Her, and She opened my heart and started to do her work. When Shakti claims you prepare for the most profound transformation you could ever possibly undergo.

Shakti changes our physiology; She makes us a fit vessel to receive the Infinite. Shakti is the physiology; She is the very structure we call ourselves – mind, body, and intellect- and She is the fire that transforms the structure. She is the transmission carried by these words. She is also contained in any resistance to these words. She creates the Universe, and She sustains the illusions within us. Her Maya is her Lila or play. And when She is ready for us to evolve, She wakes us up. If we can become aware of the power of Shakti, it will become easier for us to open to it. To fall in Love with Her and feel Her presence within you and all around you is the most rarefied of relationships. And it is Love that deepens and strengthens the awareness of Her.

Shakti is also incredibly ruthless. Don't ever underestimate Her. She will annihilate you, and then She will eat you for breakfast. She doesn't hesitate to bring down Her sword when needed. But there is something in the process of demolition that allows us to glimpse a great Love. This great Love is the love that Mother has for Her entire creation, and She wants us to be free and happy. But Mother plays, and this is Her play of consciousness. Her mystery is why some can open and receive Her, and others simply stop at some place along the way. If your heart is open to

Her, and Love for Her is what guides you and motivates you, you will keep going. But don't wait for Her to do it. It is up to us to make the effort to keep that fire of devotion burning hot. Shakti inspires us to follow Her lead, and if we are open enough to leave behind all our ideas about enlightenment and spirituality, then maybe we can genuinely know Her and be a fit vessel for Her Love.

Shakti is the great initiator of the mystery. She has created the Divine blueprint and initiates the purification to change us. The purification process can be quite painful and difficult, but Shakti knows what we can handle and will take us right to the edge, again and again. Sometimes, it will feel like too much, but that which feels that way is dying out of the system. This is how Shakti dissolves the separate self, and She is the ultimate Master. She works so deeply that most of the time, we have no idea of the changes that are taking place. These changes occur deep within the unconscious, where we cannot see or control them. She removes the controller so that we can come closer to the realm of complete surrender.

Some people may have had an initial awakening of kundalini somewhere in their journey. Openings of kundalini can be compelling as the serpentine of consciousness uncoils and begins to open our system. All kinds of crazy energy can be released, and it can be helpful to talk to someone who knows about kundalini if this is happening to you. Kundalini openings can create all kinds of extreme experiences, and because of this, it is common for the separate self to think that something special is happening. Kundalini can open a little bit, or it can open a lot. It can open the heart and clear the nadis (junctions) within the nervous system.

When I first met Amma, and my devotion finally had a form to focus on, Kundalini's play started to dance. I would go down to the Kali temple every morning and sit before Amma while She gave

Darshan. And as soon as I sat down and closed my eyes, the dance would start. I would see the form of Amma, or if my eyes were closed, I could sense Her in front of me, and I would feel a massive wave of Love arise in my being. My whole body would start to vibrate with tremendous energy. There was so much Love moving through the system that the body couldn't contain it, so it would experience strong horripilation, hair standing on end, laughing and crying and shaking all over. There would be tremendous heat in my body that would just about blow my circuits, and sweat would pour off me, drenching my clothes. The body would experience spontaneous Bandha locks (yogic energy locks), and weird Kriya movements would happen. People would tell me later that my face would be bright red. I must have looked like quite the sight because hours later, I noticed people watching me when I opened my eyes. But thankfully, due to Amma's grace, I didn't desire to "own" any of these experiences. It felt like a lot of energy and Love, and until that Love culminated in final self-realization, I wasn't interested in what was happening. I seemed to know that all this energy was the result of enormous Love in the system, and the mind knew this as well, so it wasn't getting hung up on it. This energetic opening went on for several years and felt quite good. It felt like a big flush of Love through the system, leaving me clear and refreshed. The experiences also inspired me because Shakti was working on a deep level of deconditioning, which some folks call depersonalization. Mother had begun to bring up many of my illusions and was burning me in the fire of her Love. Without the inspiration of Divine Love flowing through my system, I might not have made it through some of the complex challenges to come.

If Shakti or Mother has visited your consciousness in any way, I invite you to be curious about Her. Try to find out what She is and how to have a relationship with Her. Having a relationship sounds dualistic, but you will only know complete surrender once you are in a relationship with the Divine. An authentic and sincere relationship with Shakti is a relationship with the Supreme power transforming your physiology. See if you can feel Her deep inside your being as a gentle (or firm) pulse of Divine intelligence. Shakti is a process; She is the impulse that, if we are open to it, can transform our physiology on the deepest levels. She can transform us at the deepest core into an embodiment of Her Love.

I have seen many people who were devoted to Amma change radically over the years. I have also seen many people with Amma stay mostly the same for years. I always wonder about this. The Mother of the Universe is not a mother that tells you what to do or not do; it is up to the individual to find the pulse of Shakti within themselves and open to it. In my relationship with Amma, love and surrender kept me on a steady journey of purification so that Shakti could transform the system according to her design. We don't know what She has in store for us; we have no idea about the latent design within our physiology. Feeling her steady pulse within as She does Her work and staying quiet and receptive to her presence and intelligence is crucial. Shakti is felt, but She is not known. She is utterly inaccessible if we want to hold onto Her in any way. She may even stay hidden for a while, which can be intensely disconcerting if you are devoted to Her.

I remember a few summers while working in the States, I could not feel her with me at all. Those were tough years, as I felt tossed around without anything to hold onto. It was a very dark period for me, and I felt like Amma had left me. It was so awful. She would ignore me completely when I was with her in the ashram. She never even looked at me for two years in a row. If She saw me coming, she would turn around and walk in the other direction! She wouldn't give me the slightest glance, and I became desperate for Her. It was so painful, but now I recognize it was another way She was opening my system for her work. I remember feeling like I had been totally abandoned, and all my longing was left hanging in an empty void. It was so difficult, but the intense love kept me going. I couldn't stop. I was driven to know the Beloved–even if it cost me my life. And that is what it felt like at times–like I was losing my life. I was losing my old life–the life I used to be. Shakti was changing me radically from deep inside my core personality. I could not prepare myself for Her- She had to do it. Most of the time, She was unpredictable, and I remember feeling afraid of how she would appear. But this was the separate self that was afraid, and Amma was triggering it big time. She would shift from a blissful Motherly presence to a dark, fierce Kali just to purify and transform the system and destroy what was in the way. Whatever was needed, She would manifest.

Shakti knows what She is doing, so be wise and stay out of Her way. Amma used to say she was like a surgeon performing a highly complex surgery on each of us. Would we want to move about while She cuts? We must find our unique relationship with Shakti, the power of transformation and enlightenment. It is She who is operating; it is She who is opening the physiology and removing all the painful illusions within. If you think the personal "you" is doing the work, your chances for significant change are greatly diminished. The deeper our relationship with Shakti, the more faith we will have in our process. The more faith we have, the more open we are. This might take years, so find patience. The more we mature, the humbler we become as we recognize Her grace in our most profound transformations. The more we mature, the more we feel Her breathing light into our bodies, hearts, and intellect. It is Her power that goes in and changes our brains and neurological networks. I have experienced this to a great degree. It is all Her. We become an instrument for Her to use as She sees fit. We cease to have ideas about what being an instrument should look like or what it means. We become the witness to the process of embodiment. She will bestow wisdom, deep mystical insights, and informational downloads only when we are emptied of personal agendas and beliefs. The true mystic has a profound relationship with the power of Shakti, the Original, Supreme power of all.

9.

True Devotion

*In people with devotion, even with limited intellect,
the intellect is not making mischief.*

~Sri Nisargadatta Maharaj

*F*or many years, my body has known the grip of uncertainty. I've never had a "career," but I find little day jobs in my local area to keep my life afloat while prioritizing my spiritual journey. This grip of uncertainty will get quite intense at times due to the tenuous appearance of my life. Uncertainty can sometimes bring deep terror as the fear of survival takes hold. This body knows quite a bit of stress—as the fight-flight response to survive automatically gets triggered due to outer circumstances. These constant stress hormones will later cause some rather debilitating physical symptoms in my body, which will lead me down a different journey of Neuroscience and a deeper understanding of the mind-body connection. I will write more about this in my next book. But for now, I want to continue to share what I went through from the early years, 1994 up to 2015.

Fear and anxiety are not new; I have grown somewhat accustomed to these feelings as I continually go deeper into the unknown. The fear comes *and goes, but I have noticed a pattern as I go deeper into the unknown: fear becomes an open door for the infinite to enter. I take a little time to offer the fear some space. A strong presence enters my body as I sit and allow these feelings some space to breathe. This presence fills my body with energy, opening it up. As it opens the body up, it fills it with feelings of love and deep appreciation. It is as if presence is thanking the body for allowing it to be a vessel for the Infinite. My body feels comforted and begins to relax, and the sense of doubt disappears. The fear is still there, but much less now, and there is also a sense in the body that it knows it is doing the right thing and must keep going. This may be what courage is.*

For many years, I've had a subtle expectation for my spiritual process to find some resolution, but instead, I keep encountering a more profound realm of the unknowable. Deeper and deeper, my mind cannot even imagine what life will look like tomorrow or next week. The grip of uncertainty in the body has taken on a familiarity I cannot dismiss, so I have included it in my love affair with the Beloved.

Yet I also feel a sense of wonder welling up; I am at a perfect place where anything can happen if I remain open. My body feels aliveness flowing through its veins. I "know" I am right where I need to be—I feel aligned with the Totality deep within my physiology. And even though the mind feels unsettled at times (of course), I wouldn't want what is happening to be different in any way. I know that the incredible intelligence of life has brought me to this stopped place, and I can sense the profound preciousness of what is taking place. I can feel the depth of silence inviting me in, and the vast field of consciousness feels more significant and more vital. I sense the gift of Grace that lies within not knowing.

There is something in me that is stronger than fear, and that is an impulse to keep going. It is devotion to my process; it is devotion to the Presence that is opening the system, deep within my being. It is devotion to what guides me beyond the need to know and the mind's need for security.

I feel this devotion in my heart, guiding me to discover what is on the other side of a deep relinquishing of the known. So, as I write, you and I are on a journey of discovery, and maybe by the time this book is done, I will have something different to share.

Meanwhile, while I sit here and write, I know this is the only thing I should do. Everything else will resolve itself, and I have no idea how it will look. I sense this in my being and can only live here now. I am not doing this for myself. The eternal is living through me. The infinite tells this body-mind to let go of its need to know. To let go so much that something else can happen. So, that is what I feel–I feel a pure devotion to that which is asking this of me, and because I have come so far on the journey, I know I must keep going.

I have begun to feel the guidance of the internal Presence shifting from needing to know to not needing to know. This guidance comes from what I call a New Self, and I play back and forth between the separate self and the New Self, noting the shift of difference. The New Self feels alive, calm, strong, capable, yet completely void of identity. There is no person in the New Self. There is no fear. I go through my day with eyes wide open, shifting back and forth, and as I do this, the New Self takes over. She feels more embodied and more reliable. The old self slowly fades, only showing up when triggered, but even the triggers feel empty. My nervous system seems calmer and more aligned with the New Self. It feels safe. The nervous system seems more devoted to the New Self, shifting from needing to know to accommodating the New Self.

One of the most valuable qualities of the heart is the attitude of true devotion. True devotion is the wellspring of Grace, where our whole being is offered to a higher level of consciousness. It is the opportunity to fall deeply and totally in Love every minute of every day. Because devotion is so widely misunderstood here in the West, I would like to introduce you to its most profound meaning.

When it is felt as either longing or love, true devotion is the truth of our being, our deepest essence, longing for Itself. It is the purest consciousness calling to itself, and when we begin to experience this calling from within, it is sensed in our heart as something real and coming from truth. Consciousness is using our mind-body to long for itself. We may begin to sense the pulse of this love and a longing to live a life from this Love. This calling feels pure and is sensed in every cell of our being. If we can allow ourselves to open to true devotion, we will feel this energy in our whole body. Our lives will become an impulse to know the Divine.

Our nervous system is made to know Love, and when this system feels Love, it naturally opens to it, just like it would to human love. Experiencing true devotion is like encountering the deepest desire of our hearts- it is fulfillment even if we have not realized what we long for. The experience of devotion is the deepest satisfaction. It is the desire to open to and connect with something bigger than our small sense of ourselves, thereby losing ourselves. It is what is true within us, opening to Itself, until all illusion of separation is dissolved. The deepest desire is to know our true Self entirely and offer our lives to that Self, over and over again.

Devotion is a feeling; it is simply an opening of the heart to something bigger than what we see around us. We sense an unseen Divine Presence all around us, for the same presence within us makes us aware of this outside, infinite presence. This presence is responding to itself. This conscious presence can long to know Itself with great intensity, and to experience this in your being is a huge blessing. We can feel this in our physiology as an inexhaustible drive to know the Beloved, and this intense longing can show up in your being without any warning. It will and can take you by utter surprise!

Of course, there are many different expressions of Devotion, and they can be somewhat superficial or very deep. On a deeper level, it can feel as if the Beloved is demanding everything from us, asking that we devote our entire lives to offering our whole being to the Divine. This is service to the Divine, and it is a very high calling.

The path of devotion is not a lesser path, for in its fullest expression, it is complete and total Self-Realization. And it is not for the weak or faint of heart, because Love will take us beyond any secure arrival point. There is nothing in it for "me." But the blessing of experiencing a fully blooming presence of Divine Love pulsing within our hearts is a rich reward. And when we feel this quality of Love guiding us on our journey, everything else in life pales in comparison.

It might feel like the small "me" is longing for the truth, but the real inspiration comes from our true essence. The small "me" cannot initiate True Devotion because we will surrender everything it wants or is attached to. If the separate self practices a superficial devotion and wants something from it, that devotion will not go beyond the known and will not last unless it evolves into True Devotion. The attachments of the separate self are too strong, and the grace of pure devotion has not awakened in the heart. But anything can happen, and things can change!

Devotion can give us the added blessing of humility as we continually offer ourselves up to that higher level of consciousness. The entire human being gets offered up, where a profound transformation can occur. When the entire being is offered, the Beloved can have free reign to expose every little belief within that maintains the separation of the false self. The Beloved wants access to everything within the unconscious and will expose everything if given the chance.

She will ask that we open to our frail humanness and be honest with Her. We are not here to become an improved, separate self but to recognize that we are being opened by something that is not definable. She is beyond definition and ownership of any kind. She opens us enough to reveal how we still think of ourselves as separate individuals. All the subtleties of separation are waiting to be exposed, and most of the time, these subtleties are comprised of fears and insecurities because that is what separation creates.

Without devotion, the heart can stay closed for a lifetime. We may think our hearts are open as we feel love towards our family and friends. But if we have yet to offer our entire being to the Divine, chances are that the spiritual heart has not opened enough to access a deeper intelligence. To have our hearts open is an unforgettable experience, as our entire being becomes flooded with Divine love and unworldly knowing. When the spiritual heart opens, oftentimes, our body cannot handle all the Love flowing through it and will experience high states of ecstasy and bliss. These are all by-products of being opened by the Beloved, and she will open those ready to offer everything to Her.

Even if we have a solid intellectual understanding of awakening and have experienced some wonderful openings within consciousness, the spiritual heart can still be closed. Amma says devotion is vital for Westerners because many people are stuck in their intellects, and their hearts remain very protected. I invite you to explore the realm of feeling with your heart. Initially, it may feel like there is no energy at all, but with practice, activating the spiritual Heart can awaken the dormant energies within.

Since the nervous system is a feeling, sensing organ, an opened, activated Heart can assist in its evolution. When activated, the Heart begins to emit a profoundly rich intelligence that can inform the brain of what is true and what is not. The Heart and brain work together and become coherent, working as one unit. This coherence creates vital discernment, which is essential for Self-Realization. If we cannot discern what is true and not, we will remain trapped in ignorance and confusion.

When the spiritual Heart has been opened through devotion, it can grow wide enough to include the entire physical structure of body and mind. Because the spiritual Heart is not a physical structure, but rather an energetic one, its capacity to grow is infinite. When we feel love with the spiritual heart, the nervous system feels love throughout the whole system. When we give all of ourselves through strong devotion to the Beloved, the entire system becomes that offering. When we offer up all of ourselves, pure consciousness responds, and it does so by waking up within the nervous system. And the nervous system responds by opening to accommodate the new awakening. It is an entirely inside job, which is funny because so many think devotion is a dual-natured attitude and path. It can be in the beginning stages, which I experienced profoundly early on. It was a wonderful experience that I look back at with amazement and gratitude. But I am talking about the non-dual nature of embodied devotion: Oneness.

The nervous system is stimulated through directly feeling Love, and it feels itself longing with an intensity that automatically removes any obstructions to the awakening of consciousness within it. It becomes a vehicle to further its own evolution. The entire physical structure begins to awaken out of the personal "me" and begins to sense within its system that "bigger" something to which it gave Itself. Consciousness is waking up to Itself within the physical, and the system opens to accommodate the infinite Field of reality or a New Self.

Giving ourselves to something bigger or higher allows a tremendous opportunity for our minds to fall in love. When the mind knows Divine Love, there is nothing that it wants more than that love. It understands the precious value of Divine Love. The mind feels the truth of devotion, so whenever we encounter another layer of insecurity and fear, the mind already knows what it wants. The mind knows it can't understand its true nature until it surrenders to the ever-expanding spiritual Heart. It won't be content until it becomes one with the very source of Divine Love.

As the mind begins to recognize this, it starts to cooperate by recognizing its capacity to let go; it surrenders its need to control, and the pure light of consciousness begins to wake up within the mind. This relinquishing of control is necessary for evolution. The mind relaxes when it develops this capacity to surrender its need for control and its need to stay safe. Awareness operates through the mind, revealing the old ways of thinking that it knows, and it begins to see that it *can't know.* This pivotal time is the crux for total and complete surrender, when the mind begins to trust not knowing.

When the mind feels Love, it shifts to only wanting to know the Beloved. This shift begins aligning and attuning to this moment so that it can continually open to Love. The Heart now informs the mind, guiding it in a new way. Gradually, we develop a one-pointedness towards the supreme reality, guided by the Heart's consciousness. Consciousness focuses on itself; there is no more energy for the separate self. Gradually, this one-pointed devotion replaces all the old tendencies of the false, separate self, and the periods in which it ceases to exist grow longer.

Amma says this type of pure devotion is like winning the lottery on the spiritual path. We are so focused on our Beloved as the Totality that we recognize that this life will not find fulfillment until we know the Beloved. This is the True Self within us, which is pure consciousness, acknowledging that it will ultimately realize itself. This recognition is the foundation for the non-dual realization of Oneness.

If we are open enough, we can feel the presence of the Beloved inhabiting the mind-body complex to know Itself. This Love, which has opened our system for the Totality to embody our physiology, feels incredibly satisfying. We are permeated with Life's dynamic essence, the initiate of immense creativity, and the system senses this presence as a source of goodness for all. When we experience this Divine consummation within, we recognize that it has nothing to do with *us* as an individual. This is the awakening of the Infinite, for the Infinite. It is for the totality of creation.

When Love opens, we lose the tendency to be self-absorbed; we aren't so wrapped up with ourselves and all our little issues. Losing ourselves, even briefly, feels tremendously freeing because all that is left is the Beloved. We gradually lose our self-created interest in ourselves, what emotions are playing out, what others think of us, and what our future might bring. We gradually lose interest in maintaining separation.

True devotion is like travel insurance—losing ourselves through love is a powerful way to stay focused on this path. We must keep going until we know what we long to know; this is divine inspiration coming from that which longs for Itself. We can't say how deep the Beloved wants to go, but we must feel the subtle nudges to keep going. We must be honest that there is still more on the journey and that we are not "done."

This precise focus is needed to leave the paradigm of separation behind. This kind of one-pointedness will pull us through our limiting fears and insecurities. It is like riding a train that cannot leave its track but keeps going towards its destination. I have also heard it called a "rocket ship," as it is the vehicle that takes us beyond the gravitational pull of the illusory self. We are on a journey with a destination; it's already been arranged for the Beloved to know Itself. Evolution is about the pure light of consciousness longing to know itself in a never-before-way, and it is wholly devoted to Itself. If the devotion is pure, it will keep driving toward its destination. We might find we have to leave our luggage behind. We must let go of our tendencies to make the journey look a certain way. This is what the Beloved will ask of us. I have often recognized that I could not have made this journey "myself"–it was too risky, and the risk was asking too much of "my life." The Beloved is making the journey, so anything is possible.

To experience one-pointedness is a gradual process; it is another way that consciousness evolves. We may be scattered in our early stages of evolution. The important thing is to recognize the call, to feel in your heart that the Beloved is calling. It will look different for all of us; the essential thing is that we keep focusing on that call; we keep our hearts tuned to it. The call will be the guiding light; it is the voice of consciousness residing in the silence of our hearts, and it will lead us to a life beyond our previous life. And with time, the call becomes more precise, shedding many of the old life's conditions. Our lives are getting freed up to evolve into something completely new. Consciousness as Love is an unconditional Love, and so it has no beliefs or structures that it needs to abide by. As unconditional Love blooms within, the physical vessel matures and can live an unconditional Life.

Without true devotion, any openings or awakenings that have occurred can still be thwarted by the separate self. The pull of the separate self is powerful, and its need for security can close the vessel back up, preventing a complete surrender. The devotional energy that comes from Love, on what it loves, can keep the process pure and in the highest integrity. The pure devotional attitude from the heart will mature in time, and be free from personal agendas.

Intellectual, conceptual understanding cannot access this deep occupancy within your being. We need devotion to call it forth because the Totality responds to this. It's like a magnet. True devotion will culminate in absolute Oneness with the Divine. It will completely eradicate all the ignorance of the false, separate self. The Heart is unlimited in its capacity to know itself as Love, and when we experience this for ourselves, it will take us way beyond conceptual teachings. We only want to feel the Beloved occupying our being. Consciousness only wants to know itself; if we remain open, we can experience this in many ways.

I often invite people to open to prayer. Some of you think that prayer is for beginners or that it is for when we are weak. Yet an actual prayer, if allowed, is nothing more than consciousness speaking to itself. A true prayer allows the Heart to speak, say what it feels, and talk about its longing. It also provides a vehicle for the mind to become focused. Prayer shifts the intention from a messy, vague desire to a deep and precise focus. It allows us to get in touch with our deepest, purest desire; when we are in touch with that desire, we feel it as our most profound truth. It becomes a feeling we don't want to lose because it resonates deeply in the nervous system as Truth. The nervous system responds positively to prayer and accommodates those deep, heartfelt feelings. True prayer has nothing to do with what the separate self wants; that is how you can tell if it is true. It is the consciousness of the Heart praying to Itself, which can be extremely powerful.

The universe must respond when we express the heart's longing in prayer. For several years, I found the desire to pray, and I would pray softly to my Beloved in the early morning hours. It was such a sacred time. The words that came out were words I didn't know were in me. The prayers opened a depth in me that I would not have been able to access otherwise. The words themselves were a vehicle for Love; they carried the vibration of Love. They allowed the Heart to get in touch with its desire for Itself, and the feelings of the Heart inspired even deeper prayers. The prayers opened the lover to the Beloved- or the Divine- up to itself. Tears would flow as my system overflowed with Love. The tears of Love, for Love, can be the most profound cleansing of the soul. God is giving herself to herself. Eternally.

True devotion develops great courage. It is not for those looking for something for themselves, something to hang onto. The Beloved wants the lover all for Itself and will pull the lover through tests that take the lover beyond herself. The Beloved knows what it takes to dissolve separation and will stop at nothing. It will expose every single fear, subtle insecurity, and imagined infidelity of the lower mind. The Beloved wants this Life for Itself and knows how to get it with supreme intelligence. This creates a need for courage, and the vessel develops the capacity to surpass fears. It expands the capacity not to hold onto anything except the Beloved, the Eternal Self. This kind of devotion is invincible; amid challenges, devotion only strengthens. This is how the true spiritual warrior is born. She allows the Beloved to show her how strong she is and what she is made of. She allows the Beloved, or Supreme consciousness, to show herself as the Supreme Self.

10.
Openness

———◦———

Always remain a beginner.

~Sri Mata Amritanandamayi Devi

*M*y nervous system is being opened from the inside, like the blooming of a lotus. As I sit here and listen to Amma's bhajan, I feel her voice deep inside me; her voice is myself, my most authentic essence. This voice-essence informs my body and mind of its function as a vessel, and I feel my body's natural capacity to open, and my mind knows that it can have no idea what kind of experience it should be having. My whole body vibrates with a clear recognition of what the essence is doing– opening my body to accommodate the Infinite. The voice is in the middle of my head, and I can feel the voice changing the wiring inside my brain. The crown of my head is wide open, and I feel an incredible amount of light streaming in–saturating everything within with Divine energy. My whole being is supercharged with energy, and it feels like a balm for my nervous system; it feels so good. I know with every cell of my being that this is why I am here on this Earth: to be entirely available for the Infinite Being to inhabit this human body.

Amma occasionally calls herself a pipe, especially when someone praises her. If you have ever looked at her story, where she has come from, and what she is bringing into the world, you will recognize that she is a massive pipe. To be open to what is opening us is the way we become pipes, too.

Openness is the most essential part of our evolutionary process. It's an attitude. Without openness, there can be no profound change in our life experience. Being open isn't about trying to accept everything the way it is; that's just a mental construct. We rarely cooperate with what is happening if it goes against our beliefs. Instead, it is an attitude of surrendering to our internal experience so that something new can happen. When we are open, we are allowing a new consciousness to emerge. If we are not open, we remain stuck in the habituated programs from the past.

In our daily lives, outside situations will trigger us; this is how we become Aware. Triggers can help us become more open by inviting us to tune into our internal experience. Instead of blaming the external, we turn and face the internal. This is how we become conscious. If we don't do this, we operate from unconscious programs and habituated reactions. Our responses to life situations won't be conscious, and we will stay stuck in redundant energy patterns. Stuck energy patterns cause all kinds of problems, including disease. However, acknowledging our triggers and taking responsibility for them allows us to learn how to open our energy channels within the nervous system. We invite in new energies, which shift and transform our physiology, changing our perceptions of reality.

When we realize how powerful this invitation to "stay open" can be, we will start to live in a way capable of transmuting old stuck energy.

Everything can be seen as energy. Old energy creates the same circumstances over and over until we learn how to change it. Old programs from the past are simply old energy. Nothing new is happening, and if we keep doing the same thing repeatedly, we create a certain genetic destiny for ourselves. However, new energy changes the genetic signature, and the physiological change needed to become a pipe.

Amma calls this the realm of constant change; if we are serious about our evolution, this is where we want to be. These past programs are the building blocks of the separate self, and if we want to dissolve the illusions of separation, we must learn to change our energy. We must open. We must approach life with a certain attitude of humility and receptivity, a not-knowing coupled with pure devotion towards the Divine.

When our system is opened and new energy begins informing it, we begin living a life we have never lived before because the old programs no longer distort our perceptions. We are being opened beyond our old, conditioned way of perceiving. The energy is doing this, not the separate self.

Openness is like allowing a cool, fresh breeze to blow into your being; it can feel incredibly refreshing, which inspires us to remain open. And that fresh breeze begins to be recognized as a Presence that is always with you, beckoning you to go beyond yourself- beyond the self that you have always been.

If you are drawn to read this book, you may have had an experience with Presence. When we are quiet and still, there can be recognition of a Presence in the space around us. Take a moment and see if you can sense a Presence around you. Recognize it by allowing it to reveal itself. Let it come to you. Everyone has access to this recognition simply because it is always here. You don't need to have had any kind of spiritual awakening or experience to recognize Presence. Presence is always here if you just stop enough and feel it. It is a felt sense. It is not necessarily something you see. We are accessing more feelings and sensing our internal world by recognizing Presence. We are activating an aspect of our nervous system that can go deep into the subtleties of illusion.

When we sense Presence, we can open to it. Opening to Presence can be felt in the body and the nervous system. The felt sense of Presence begins a new alchemical evolution within the nervous system, which begins to transcend the experience of separation and isolation. We begin to recognize that we are not all alone here, even when we are all alone in a room. It is not something to do only when we need some stillness or want to get in some spiritual state. The recognition of Presence can be a lifelong relationship, a deep interaction that evolves over time. To begin to establish a personal relationship with Presence is extremely helpful. This relationship will become more vital as we continually open to it while letting go of our attachments and stories. It's a rich interaction with Source consciousness while remaining open and agenda-free.

Pay attention to what may come with this invitation to open to Presence. Maybe you feel silly, scared, or relieved that you finally get to share yourself. This exchange could feel deeply intimate if you can open that much. See if you can sense that Presence knows everything about you and that you can't hide anything. Can you allow yourself to be seen that deeply? Can you feel the guards drop when you are seen so thoroughly? Can you recognize that Presence has no judgment when it sees you? Can you sense that Presence sees nothing wrong? Can you sense your body responding when seen entirely without judgment? Can you recognize your body's capacity to let this Presence in, receiving Presence into every cell of your being? Can you feel there is no difference between the sense of Presence on the outside of the body and within the body? Can you feel yourself drop into this glorious moment as the pure luminosity of Presence?

The body and nervous system have a tremendous capacity to open. It is designed to open, so much so that it can go beyond its old sense of identity and form. Our system can sense that there are no borders inside and outside, that the environment around us is the same as the environment within. The essential Presence, or Field of consciousness, is the same outside as inside. The edges fade, and the more the nervous system recognizes this, the more open it becomes until the belief of an isolated physical body is dissolved. The body and nervous system are our means to sense Presence, and this is how we open to the essence of Life that is within everything and everywhere. It's about consciousness opening the body enough to receive itself. This is the foundation for the fundamental perception of unity consciousness.

An essential fundamental shift occurs during the evolutionary process, yet it is a shift that takes place over time. It begins when we, as consciousness, awaken from the belief that we are an isolated "me" living in a body and separate from the rest of Life. This is the essential shift or an authentic awakening. Then, there is a period when we don't know what we are. This period can last many years and can be disorienting for some folks. Yet, over time, we begin to adjust to the odd sense of being unable to find ourselves. To not have any ideas about ourselves and who and what we are is the beginning of being open, and for most people, a period of "ripening" takes place. In this period, we are continually being dismantled from the need to hold onto ways of knowing ourselves. Any old programs of identity simply fall away, along with the need to hold onto and manage any kind of experience. This is important. Being open means letting go of the need to maintain any experience.

We try to find ourselves in the world in many ways, defining ourselves through relationships with others or our external circumstances, careers, and pastimes. But when we become more Aware, we can see how the separate self uses the world to validate itself. This can be sobering at times and challenging, as the separate self will cling to anything to find some sort of validation. The separate self needs validation and acknowledgment. But as the separate self begins to fade, we will lose all interest in maintaining these old ways of operating. We see them as empty, void of happiness and freedom. Any clinging to or needing anything is not free. All the ways we attempt to hold onto knowing anything will be dissolved in this deepening period, sometimes unceremoniously. This maturation period is essential and prepares for the actual embodiment or change of occupancy, the blooming of consciousness within the mind-body complex.

The first essential shift was just getting our foot in the door; now, we must open it wide to continue the process. The opening within our system wants to take us beyond our habitual reference of who and what we are and what we think we know. The most significant opportunity is to drop all our ideas about awakening and "stay open." Staying open will allow all the stuck tendencies within our system to become accessible so that we can allow without resistance. When we are open, we will encounter many old tendencies, many of which are cleverly disguised. Staying open allows conscious awareness to see past these disguises, as they will become increasingly more subtle and tricky. And the deeper we go into the subtleties, the deeper consciousness awakens within the system.

Watch the temptation to hold onto popular concepts such as "there is no 'me'" or any other temptation that maintains a fixed position. This is a crucial time; the more open we can be, the deeper the maturation. This is also a time when consciousness exposes any impatience within our system; maybe the separate self wants the process to be over or doesn't see the point in continuing. These are just common hijackings of the mind. There can be no resolution in evolution. This incubation period can last decades, which is a good thing. The maturing of consciousness within the physical structure is essential if we are to evolve out of the paradigm of separation. In all honesty, even if we have experienced any kind of awakening, we can still feel separate, and the separate self can still try to maintain its "spiritualized" version of itself. Yet, given time, coupled with openness and grace, separation will lose its hold within consciousness. If we have an awakening where we have seen through the façade of a small "me," it is still essential that we remain honest about what comes up after. It might take a while for things to settle after a shift in consciousness, and you may experience some grand new perspective from the change, but consciousness will come back in and expose so much more than what you have seen. It's unbelievable how much more ignorance can be seen in the ever-evolving system as it goes deeper into the unconscious.

I have seen quite a bit in my years as a teacher, and it helped me understand the many trickeries of the separate self. Some folks may have their first essential shift and then think they are ready to begin teaching, or they may think they know something and are now here to help humanity. This is extremely common. I have also watched folks get angry when they weren't recognized as an "awakened" person, and instead of getting curious about the source of their anger, they found me at fault for not seeing them as "awakened." I have seen folks get stuck in the concept that there is no "me," and the rest doesn't matter. Many current Western spiritual teachings support this shallow approach to evolution, where awakening is the end goal, not authentic Self-Realization or Embodiment. The pure teachings under the guidance of a genuine Master aren't valued in the West like they are in traditional settings, so the teachings become distorted and watered-down. They lose their immense power of profound transformation. The pure teachings of the Sanatana Dharma carry the transmissions of the great rishis of ancient times. Their standard was very high. Why would we want to lower it? Only the false, separate self would distort the pure teachings and adopt a lower standard to accommodate its own agenda.

It's risky; anything can happen, and some people can slow their evolution after an awakening. Many folks may hold onto a shift simply because it feels much better than where they came from. They unconsciously believe that moving beyond might bring them more suffering, so they tend to "hold" onto the awakening by attempting to maintain some experience. This is quite common. But sooner or later, not moving beyond will also cause suffering, and the pain of separation will return- because it never really left. At any rate, given time, the fantastic wonder of that initial shift will become a faded memory, and life will demand authenticity. But what we gain from that initial awakening is the capacity to see more, from Awareness. Awakening can clear our lens and make it wider. But we must nurture the lens, not the memory of a shift. The folks who do not open beyond the initial shift tend to stagnate and may go back to sleep due to a lack of devotion. They will hold onto the remembrance of their awakening, but the old stuck programs still control the personality, and ignorance remains.

That initial shift gifts us with something that we can never forget. It can also propel us forward on our journey to a great degree. We will know that something is waking up within us that isn't "us." This is where devotion shines, where we can see that offering this life, mind, and body is what this journey is about.

I have seen much in my years of teaching about the nature of the false ego self and how it maintains its separation. I have seen in myself how the false ego self attempts to hang onto anything that will give it some way of finding resolution with itself. Seeing these tendencies in ourselves takes tremendous awareness, devotion, and honesty. Our evolutionary process can take us beyond any fixed reference and into any need for one. We lose any interest or need to be anyone at all. An "awakened" experience is just another reference point. So, you can imagine how there can be infinite ways for the separate self to hold on. This is why it is so essential that we stay open. Just stay open…and ask yourself, "What keeps trying to keep itself separate?" "What keeps needing to be validated?" And then stay open to what is revealed.

The separate self is, by its very nature, fearful. It is terrified of losing its sense of personal existence. These feelings are all created in the brain through memories of the past- of being a separate self. The funny thing is that when we are curious about our sense of fear, we find it completely ungrounded- like there isn't anything to be afraid of. It's a distorted perception. This is one of the ways to begin distinguishing unconscious programs and start opening to them. We are opening the gate to the unconscious by becoming aware of its false habituated perceptions.

Fear is not bad; it tells us when the separate false self wants to find a place to hold onto. If we stay curious about fear, we can remain open. But we cannot be open if we ignore fear. If fear is kept at a distance or managed in any way, it keeps our system from opening. Fear feels tight and contracted. Staying open, even with fear, allows the spaciousness of consciousness to enter. And the more open we are, the more fear consciousness will expose. When the separate self is dissolving, and all its references are being stripped away, you can count on fear being present in your system. Fear can get quite intense as we stop propping up the separate self. Pay attention to those little thoughts trying to convince you everything will be okay. This is just the mind keeping us from going deep into the unconscious programs. It might not be okay; you don't know. Staying open to fear is another way to open the system. Feel it and open to it. Allow it fully. Again and again. It only means the separate self is hanging on for its dear life.

I have had tremendous amounts of fear reveal itself in my system. Of course, my life has been focused on the Divine rather than creating material security, which was necessary for me. Because of this, the fear of the separate self compounded greatly, which became deeper invitations to let go and open. It hasn't been easy living with so much fear, and there was a period where it was repressed because it was too much for me to handle. This caused some problems temporarily, but through grace, consciousness moved into fear and allowed it when the time was right.

The more mature and open we become, the more we want to see every illusion within our system. And if we want to see it all, we will. This gives us great humility. We recognize that we are not an "awakened person" or "special." We get to see that we are essentially nothing identifiable! One of Amma's most well-known quotes is, *"When we become a zero, then we can become a hero."* Feel free to interpret this for yourself. I have never heard of Amma calling herself enlightened, and I have also never seen her call anyone else enlightened! From her perspective, no one is enlightened; only one true reality exists. As we mature, we recognize that the spiritual process is about our systems being opened and transformed by consciousness. And the degree to which we are open is relative to our willingness to be nobody. It's another safety mechanism within the design of evolution.

Try not to interpret your process in any way, such as putting yourself somewhere along some linear advancement towards some imaginary endpoint. Often, people want to know where they are in the scheme of enlightenment, but the truth is, you can't say. Sometimes, it does help the mind to get on board to understand the process, but beyond that, there is no point other than to try and find yourself somewhere. When you stop needing to know, you can be open. If you want some reference points, you cannot be open to what is here right now.

Identification with the body is one of the last holdings that consciousness dissolves, as it is the most substantial reference for the separate self to hold onto. We can invite the body to open to Presence in an everyday way; this allows some space to penetrate the identification. Amma says that identification with the body is dense and is usually the last to go. So please don't despair when you recognize that physical identification is still quite strong for you. Don't try to deny the body in any way, but don't give it any preference, either. It is an instrument or vehicle and should not be given any extra energy as this strengthens identification. Giving the body special preference is just another *vasana*, which can cause endless cycles of delusion. The important thing is to stay open and to be where you are authentically.

When we open to Presence, it is like opening a window and letting fresh air in. The nervous system in the body feels it and naturally responds to it by opening because it feels so good. Our body and nervous system are designed to accommodate Presence, and the system becomes increasingly more sensitive through its contact with Presence. They were made for each other. Meditation can also foster sensitivity within our system. If we are relaxed and open during meditation, and there is no personal drive to get a particular experience, our system becomes a vessel for a vibrating living Presence.

During the embodiment process, Presence has a quality of descending. It descends into the depths of the unconscious as a more profound and subtle awareness. The more the separate self is out of the way, the deeper this Aware Presence can penetrate the nervous system. Regular meditation can be incredibly healing for the nervous system simply because of the deepening of Presence within.

For some of you, devotion can be beneficial here: try sensing this Presence to be your own Beloved or something you long to know intimately. You sense that Presence knows you like no other and expects nothing from you in any way. Feel Presence waiting for you to open; feel Presence to be a friend that will never leave you. The body and heart naturally open to the Beloved like a lover. When we open to Presence, it is the invitation for the Beloved to enter completely and consume us. The Beloved Presence can then softly inform the body of what is true in their silent language. The body feels cared for from within; we feel love and appreciation coming from the inside. The body's natural response to this deep conversation is to let go and relax, and the body can recognize deep relaxation as its natural state; it forgets that it is a separate self. The feeling of Presence within the nervous system evolves organically into Presence sensing itself; consciousness knows itself as the Beloved Presence. The Beloved Presence invites us to offer all our being, and we can feel a blissful delight in this play of consciousness. This play begins with simply being open, and staying open to the Beloved can take us far beyond ourselves.

Our physical body begins to feel this aliveness of Presence in the marrow of its bones and in the movement of its blood. This feeling can begin to relax all our old tendencies that distract us from being present. The body's recognition of Presence within allows it to sense that it, too, is part of Presence, opening even more profoundly. The Presence within the physiology begins to sense itself everywhere, which negates the identification with a separate self. The physical body evolves as consciousness because it was made to evolve, and its evolutionary process takes us beyond our experience of being separate. The body has become a pipe. We cannot know the infinite possibilities within this paradigm until separation is gone. We cannot access those more profound realms of knowing until there is no one left to own the knowing.

When the body feels like a pipe or a vessel, it has nothing left to do but be open to the wonder of this moment. It feels the fingers typing these words; it feels itself being breathed, and it waits until the inner aliveness moves it again. Sensing this happening within you can be wondrous, but no one is fascinated by it. No one needs to know where this is all going. The most important thing is to keep being aware of this new paradigm- being an instrument of the Divine.

Because this process is so natural, it will feel like a flow- a natural opening of something very quiet and precious that you would never want to disturb in any way. We sense the sacredness of a deep communion within our being. And because we recognize how precious it is, we maintain its integrity. I invite you to see your process as incredibly precious; feel the rare sanctity of the communion within your being -the communion of Presence and the body. The source of the Universe has given you this moment to recognize this essential truth. Stay open and let this recognition bloom like a lotus flower within your being.

You may find yourself wondering where all this is headed, and if the wondering is innocent and impersonal, you can stay open and align with this moment. All is well, even when it isn't perfect. We sense a profound mystery unraveling, and we know that the mystery is unfolding within us. If we remain open, we can meet each moment with an attitude of wonder and awe. We stay open to what is relevant now, in this moment, and in doing so, we invite in the magic.

11.
Integrity and the Teacher

Grace comes out of nowhere.
It can happen anytime, in any place.

~Sri Mata Amritanandamayi Devi

*I*t is 1993, and I just lost my very best friend, my dog. She went everywhere I went and was at my side through many challenging times,
including the passing of my mom at a very young age. I feel a big gaping
hole inside my heart and a deep need to fill it with something good.

I am currently living in southwest Colorado. Since I feel like I have
lost a family member, I have decided to take a trip to California to visit
my grandmother, who lives in the San Francisco Bay Area. On my way
there, I see a poster with a picture of Ammachi and an invitation to come
see her. Amma is going to be offering public programs in East Bay during
the time I am visiting my grandma. I am not currently looking for a
teacher in any way. For the past several years, I have felt close to another
female Indian saint, Mother Meera, and even though I've never met this
"Mother" physically, I have a great love for her. If I did meet my "Mother,"
I feel I would not survive- my love for her is that strong.

There are only a few folks around when I arrive at the M.A. ashram grounds in San Ramon. It is between the morning and evening programs, so I pull into the parking lot, get out of my truck, and start messing with my stuff in the back camper. The ashram is located among beautiful rolling hills, and vast canopies of oak trees give shade in the dirt parking lot. I glance over at a group of 5 or 6 people standing in a circle near where I am parked. I can see that they are looking at a photograph, and as I move closer, I can see it is a picture of Mother Meera. I want to hear what they say, so I walk over to them and introduce myself. I tell them I have never met Ammachi before, but I consider the woman in the photo my "Mother." A woman immediately responds by telling me that both "Mothers" have the same energy that has taken birth in different forms. I immediately feel drawn to these people, and the woman takes me under her wing, shows me the temple, and ensures I will have a place to sit up front. She tells me I am a "newbie," so I get to sit close to Amma when she comes in.

When the time comes for the evening program to start, I find myself eagerly anticipating Amma's arrival. I've been told about Amma by some close friends who have received her Darshan. They said her Darshan was remarkable and that they try to see her whenever possible. I feel open to meeting Amma because of all the sadness in my heart. So, when Amma walks into the temple amidst beautiful chanting, I feel my heart open in her presence. Amma walks by, and I experience a sweet fragrance that has nothing to do with the scent of anything. Amma is about 4'10" tall and very dark-skinned. She walks up to the stage and bows down to everyone in the hall with incredible sweetness. Then she sits down on her little raised platform and starts gazing and smiling at everyone. There is a tangible sense of Presence that seems to have captivated the entire hall of people. The focus feels very intense. This is precisely what I was hoping for. Amma continues to smile so lovingly at everyone, but she never looks once at me. I can't help but wonder about this, so I tell myself it is because she is breaking down my ego. I hear my mind tell me that this is a good thing. I will not let it bother me that she's not looking at me.

The program begins with talks from Amma and a swami, and then the music called Bhajans begins. I can't believe how much power there is in the room as the entire hall sings with Amma. I feel like I am being transported into another dimension and lose all sense of myself. My whole being experiences a complete energy transformation as the mystical melodies take over. After the bhajans, there is a short meditation, and then Amma starts receiving people for her Darshan. After the bhajans are finished, I feel like I can't even move, so I sit transfixed, watching the Darshan take place. I feel like something extraordinary is going on, but I can't describe it.

I am told that when you want to get Darshan, you should get in line. About a couple hundred people are here tonight, and Amma is taking time with each person as they approach her. She is holding them for long periods and gazing at each person very lovingly. Sometimes, she strokes people's backs as they lie in her lap and wipes people's tears away as they spontaneously open to her. As I watch Amma give these lengthy Darshans to people, I sense she is doing much more than just hugging people. I watch each recipient get up from her lap, and often, they are blissed out or rise with tears streaming down their cheeks. Amma's presence seems to open peoples' hearts naturally, and I feel my tears beginning to well as I relax. After sitting there for several hours, I feel my heart calling me to the Darshan line, and I walk over and sit down in the line. It feels like a pre-Darshan is going on in the line as something in myself is getting ready to receive the Darshan. We all scoot along the floor closer and closer. When I reach the spot in front of Amma, her attendants gently guide me close to Amma. Amma briefly holds me in her arms, whispers something in my ear, and then lets me go. She doesn't even look at me! My Darshan must be the fastest and least affectionate out of all the Darshans I have seen tonight! But I feel something going on, so I go find a place to sit and close my eyes. Once again, I tell myself that Amma has given me a short Darshan because my ego needs it. I accept this as I watch Amma give Darshan through the night, lavishing each person with so much Love.

The next day is another program, and I am eager to sit in Amma's presence again. Once again, she ignores me as she looks lovingly around the room, and again, I tell myself it is because of my ego. When it is time to get Darshan, I feel prepared to be blessed. And again, my Darshan is the shortest one of the day, and Amma doesn't even look at me when she releases me. Again, I tell myself it is because of my ego. This pattern is repeated over the next few days. It feels like Amma is completely ignoring me, so I keep telling myself it is because of my ego. At the end of the San Ramon programs, Amma walks out of the hall and into a waiting car, and I feel my heart go with her. I feel a quiet dissatisfaction inside, knowing I must see Amma again.

The next place I see her is in Santa Fe, New Mexico, where some devotees have donated a big chunk of land for Amma to hold her programs. We are in a big tent up in the hills, surrounded by pinon and juniper trees. The program is relatively small as we sit and wait for Amma to arrive. I feel both anticipation and apprehension at the thought of seeing Amma again, and as I wait for her to enter, I kneel with my head bowed in silent prayer. I can feel the energy shift as Amma walks into the tent. She slowly walks through the small crowd, walks right up to me, stops, puts her hand on top of my head, and pushes down really hard! Then she walks away and up onto the stage.

Amma looks out at the group of her children and gazes at each person so lovingly, except me. She never looks at me, not even for a second. I feel something crack inside me as all my reasons fall apart. I want Amma to look at me! I want to feel Amma's love, too! I am beginning to feel a longing well up inside as I have never felt before; all the love I have given in my prayers over the years and the intense work I have done on myself during those years in Sedona, everything starts to bubble up from inside. Amma still doesn't look at me, and I can't stand it for another minute. I quickly gather my things and walk out of the tent. As I leave the tent, sobs begin to bubble up, and I start to lose control. A few people look at me with concern as I rush out as fast as possible. Fortunately, trees nearby will hide me, and I slow down as I find myself out of sight and earshot. Being in the trees feels so good; they feel like my friends. I see a secluded spot to sit down, and then I give in to pure, intense emotion. All my pretending that not being looked at didn't bother me cracks wide open, and I feel intense longing arising. My longing for the Divine Mother is a raging, fierce love; now that it has been opened, it burns hot. The sobs are wracking my entire being as my little group of trees hold a loving space for me. All I want is God; all I have ever wanted is God. Doesn't God know this? I have given up so much for my spiritual search, and now I am being completely ignored. The futility of this endeavor is not lost on me, yet longing is what is happening, so I let it rage through me.

After many hours of crying with the trees, I get something to eat out of my truck. I now feel entirely drained; I don't know what I feel. I must go back in and see Amma, so I wash my face and wait until the evening program starts. As I wait with everyone else for Amma to enter the tent, I feel a new inner stillness and a deep relinquishing of any need for pretense. All I know is that I want God, and anything else feels wrong. As Amma walks in, I don't feel any eagerness or apprehension; I feel empty and open. She takes her place on her peetham and begins to look around. As she is gazing at everyone, she glances at me from the side and has a little knowing smile. She sees me.

I still feel empty and reticent when I go up for Darshan. I do not know what I need for my ego or spiritual path. I do know that I want Amma to hold me, though. I want to know Amma's love deeply. When I kneel before her, she takes me in her embrace, tucks me under her arms, and holds me there for a long, long time. She strokes my back, and I feel she knows everything about me: My past, thoughts, flaws, and shortcomings. None of it matters to her. As she holds me, it feels like she is absorbing me. It feels boundless and endless. Eternal. She looks lovingly into my eyes when she releases me and says, "Good girl."

Amma is only in Santa Fe for two days, so the next day, I get used to being in Amma's presence differently. I recognize that staying open and not knowing what we need is the way to receive Amma—being present and open with her means feeling precisely what is happening and not trying to feel something that is not happening. All my preconceived ideas had blocked me and my first meeting with Amma, yet through her incredible transformative presence, She showed me what was there in me: a deep longing for God.

After Amma leaves, I head into the mountains above Santa Fe on a little overnight backpacking trip. I sleep up high, and in the evening, as I sit looking out over the vastness of the desert, I know without a doubt that I am going to India. And I will sell my little Toyota truck to get there; I need to be with Amma.

We are all unique expressions of the Divine, so finding your own journey is essential. There is no way anyone's process will look like mine- thank goodness! Allowing your journey to unfold in its perfect authenticity is a beautiful way for the Infinite to express itself. Your path might take you in a completely different direction than what everyone else is doing. Follow it! You might have to find great courage and be honest with yourself, questioning if you are following the sheep while perhaps recognizing that it isn't working for you. Your journey might not look extraordinary from the outside, and perhaps you live an everyday life. This doesn't mean that your process can't take you deep. Your process should potentially be able to take you beyond yourself, so if you wish for a "showier" process and are not getting it, this, too, can wear down any false images you may be harboring. Your current path may or may not have a teacher; just be clear about whether you have any beliefs about the need for a teacher. Because you don't know what your path should look like, and nor do I!

In 2007, when I started offering meetings in my little house, I noticed that some people were coming to Satsang with an idea about what Satsang should be. Some folks thought we should be working on our emotional stuff, and some thought I should teach from a completely non-dual perspective. These expectations were all coming from people who had been to Satsang before. I have encountered many more folks who have come in the door with ideas about what they should be experiencing than those who just come in. Yet the ones that came in the door without any ideas were the ones that benefited the most. The people who experienced significant shifts were open enough because they had no expectations. They were open and unassuming, humble. They were available for something else. Those who came in with an idea about what their process should look like usually didn't last too long. No matter what I said to them, they were usually too attached to their ideas to be able to see past them.

When Amma cracked me open, I could see that staying true and honest with myself was the most essential ingredient on the path. By staying true and honest with ourselves, I do not mean that we try to find a path that fits our idea about what we need. To stay true to our process, we must move into our hearts and let go of any of our mental spiritual idealisms. If we have any ideas about what a spiritual process should look like, we are coming from our minds. Our minds cannot know what our process should look like. When we follow our journey, we can feel a subtle (or firm) impulse within us. This inner impulse can be a fantastic guidance system that can operate when we are in integrity with it. In other words, our inner guidance can lead us toward incredible transformation and growth if we stay open. If we are looking to find a popular path that fits our ideas about what a path should look like, we will probably not go beyond ourselves. If we follow our inner guidance of the heart, we will most likely find ourselves on a different path than our friends, and we will find ourselves alone. It is in aloneness that we discover intimacy with the infinite.

Of course, these aren't the rules, but we must remember that our inner guidance knows the process that will take us beyond ourselves. Our impulse comes from an intelligence that knows exactly what we need. Our minds will think we know what we need, but over time, we gain the wisdom to see that the mind can never know, and we stay open.

When I returned after being in India with Amma for nine years and began settling in the West, my inner guidance led me straight to another teacher. He was helpful at that time because he talked directly to my mind, allowing me to understand things that had happened within me. This understanding allowed the mind to cooperate with the process and wake up to what was informing it from within. Every single teacher that my inner guidance led me to was perfect at the right time. Amma was the path that led me beyond myself, and I resisted at first. But in Amma, I met a genuine true Master, a *Sat Guru*, and my inner guidance continues to lead me deeper into an eternal relationship with Her, which is Oneness with Her.

When we follow our inner guidance, we will be led beyond what our world dictates. This may not look different on the outside, but on the inside, we come from completely different operating systems. We are being led beyond the need for security and approval. We cannot go beyond ourselves if we are concerned about what others think about us. If we still need to "fit in," we cannot feel our inner guidance. This may cause us to go from one teacher to the next without deepening with any of them. Or maybe the process wants us to move on, but we stay with a famous teacher because all our friends are there. Our spiritual journey is about autonomy, and our soul leads us beyond any popular trends. We must learn to listen to this call.

Your inner guidance is the genuine impulse of your inner teacher. Most people need an outer teacher until the inner teacher can be trusted. It is not that the inner teacher is untrustworthy; it is just that we do not know how to differentiate our inner teacher from our conditioned mind. The mind can feel like a genuine impulse in a particular direction when it is only the mind thinking it knows what it needs. If we follow our mind's projection, we will miss the inner teacher's impulse. The mind might also convince us that we do not need a teacher, yet the inner guidance might very much want an outer teacher. The mind cannot access the deep wisdom of the inner teacher, which is why the outer teacher is irreplaceable. It is only much later in our process that the mind becomes absorbed into the inner teacher that it can begin to understand things differently. This is where we will find a high standard of integrity in our process. That integrity will be significantly tested, for the inner teacher wants complete authority. The inner teacher will take us beyond all our beliefs about life, and we will leave our separate selves behind in the process. The inner teacher takes us on a journey that we can't imagine, so we begin to pay attention much differently. We are leaving behind an old reality without *anything* to hold onto.

The inner teacher is a deep intelligence that knows everything hidden within our unconscious. The inner teacher gives its voice as an intuitive feeling in the body. When we align with our inner guidance, it feels like a deep resonance, almost like a ringing bell. We are attuned. We *know* we are right where we need to be *as a feeling*. Sometimes, I feel this alignment as a ringing in my ear, signaling there is information and to pay attention.

We can slow down our process if we are not aligned with the teacher and are merely attempting to serve our belief system. If we are to go beyond ourselves, we must be willing to question every belief we have about our spiritual life. All spiritual beliefs come from the mind of the separate self because it needs something to hold onto. How can the separate self know how to go beyond itself? It's not possible. But the separate self can keep us from feeling inner or outer guidance because it has no interest in truly going beyond itself. It may have ideas about what it will look like, but it can't imagine what it actually is. Every little belief on the path can be a big obstacle because beliefs close us down. We cannot feel the inner guidance attempting to show us the way when we are closed. This is why the outer teacher is crucial for most of us.

When we are open, we attract the grace that allows us to feel the guidance within. Our openness informs the inner teacher that we do not know what our process should look like. When we are open, we are dismantling the very fabric of our belief system. When we are open, we are not the tiny, separate self but the vast, boundless field of consciousness. The infinite field of consciousness shines within the mind, and the mind gradually lets go of its need to know. When we don't know, we are dismantling the beliefs that block authentic inner guidance, allowing an authentic emergence to commence. The inner teacher will only reveal itself when the student is open and aligned with not-knowing. The inner teacher is a complete absence of knowing based on belief. She is true silence.

The vast intelligence of the infinite is felt as emerging guidance from within. Sometimes, it can be scary to follow that impulse as it leaves the familiar world behind. We leave behind all our personal expectations, hopes, attachments, and dreams—those that belong to the separate self.

But what we are left with is vibrantly alive and full of potential. It is pure life itself. By not following this guidance, you feel the redundancy of the known. You will feel the absence of inner inspiration and wonder.

Feel the difference; play with it and imagine which path is what your heart is calling you towards.

Then you will know what you want.

12.

Oh, Mind, what do you know?

Stop identifying with the world created by your mind,
and a whole new world will open up before you.

~SRI MATA AMRITANANDAMAYI DEVI

I am going up for Darshan with Amma. We are in Michigan, and a lovely program is being held over Thanksgiving. There is so much to be grateful for, and I feel very open when Amma takes me in her arms. When she releases me, she reaches for the tray of wrapped and unwrapped chocolates and pops an unwrapped chocolate in my already open mouth (we seem to know when she wants to hand-feed us.) She looks at me lovingly and sweetly says the word "baby." To be hand-fed by Amma these days is rare, but occasionally, she pops the Prasad in our mouths (usually someone hands her the Prasad in her open hand, which consists of a wrapped Hershey's Kiss and a flower petal). I sit by Amma's side, cherishing the chocolate as it slowly melts in my mouth.

The next time I go for Darshan, she again reaches for an unwrapped chocolate, but my mind jumps in uninvited and silently says, "No, you did that last time." Immediately, she puts the unwrapped chocolate in my hand along with a wrapped one. She smiles at me with a look that invites me to be very curious. I see that my mind had just blocked out the possibility of her putting the chocolate in my mouth again. The mind has just sabotaged a possibility by thinking that an event could only happen a certain way. Of course, I did not want that outcome; I would rather have had Amma hand-feed me again, but the mind's programming dictated an outcome. It made it so.

The third time I go for Darshan, I am sure I won't let myself fall for the mind's trick again. I don't want it to get in the way of my darshan with Amma! So, I go up to Amma, and again, she reaches for the unwrapped chocolates beside her. I open my mouth, and she pops the chocolate in. Then, she laughs and says something in Malayalam.

"Amma was going to give you the one wrapped in foil!" her attendant translates.

Amma laughs again and signals me to sit on the stage beside her. I walk over and sit down, feeling foolish yet knowing that Amma has given me something priceless. She just dismantled my mind.

The third time I went up for Darshan, I "thought" I knew what she was going to do, and in that "thinking," I was not open. The programming in me could only come up with a particular set of outcomes so I couldn't see any other possibility. My mind dictated the moment and made it so. In the moments following this encounter, as I sat next to Amma, I began to recognize the power that lies dormant in the mind.

We remain limited by our mind's unconscious and uninvited projections. Most of our thoughts come to us unbidden and seemingly beyond our control. Learning and watching the mind and how it creates our reality is crucial to our evolution. When we think we know what will happen based on our unconscious programming, we stay locked into an extremely limited way of experiencing Life. We remain bound.

The way that Amma played with me was priceless, beautiful, and gentle, yet highly effective. It wasn't done only as a teaching but in a way that a mother would teach her children- with love and patience. I never felt like it was a lesson or that I was in the wrong. It was playful and humorous, yet it hit home with fantastic clarity and precision. This is the way of a true Master. My mind let go, recognizing that it didn't know what would happen. It relaxed. When the mind sees that it can't know, it can relinquish the need to know. This is not just a concept to be understood but a direct experience that dismantles the unconscious grasping of the mind. In this way, the mind begins to awaken.

Much of the time, folks go around saying they don't know anything or don't know what's going to happen. However, the mind is still operating within a particular set of programs. It is still under its dictation that, given any set of circumstances, there can only be a specific set of outcomes. If we add one plus one, it can only equal two. If I do this, then the outcome will be that. The mind dictates the outcome and is not open to the unknown.

It is essential to become curious about how the mind controls our experience. This is a way to start to see how we are still locked in this three-dimensional reality based on the mind's interpretations.

The mind is incredibly powerful, and until we are free of the habituated tendencies of the mind, we cannot harness this power. We do not need to stop all our thinking; we just need to start witnessing. Through objective observation, we can become aware of how our mind can only see the reality that it *thinks*. The mind is not something we must eliminate, ignore, or bypass. This kind of approach will never purify the mind. The mind is a powerful tool in our embodiment- why would we want to push it away? Only the separate self will attempt to get rid of the mind. But the Infinite reality knows the true source of the mind and the potential of that source.

The mind is an aspect of our physiology created by the programs in our brain.. It is directly linked to the feelings that the nervous system experiences. When we have a thought, we generally have a feeling, which creates another thought, and so on. The mind and body are directly connected, which is why purification of the mind is so essential. Learning how to influence our mind is becoming a Master of our mind. There is no dismissal whatsoever, only change.

We've all experienced the power of the mind. It operates all day long, every day, often without our awareness. If we have a fearful or worrying thought, we experience a contraction in the nervous system. We try to push the thoughts away that create these feelings so that we feel good. But pushing away thoughts won't create the change that we want. It won't get into the nervous system to open it. If the thoughts are creating the feeling which creates the thoughts, then we want to learn how to begin harnessing that power so that we, as Awareness, decides what energy is needed to open the system.

The thinking mind is a survival tool for itself. It is an extension of the brain, whose sole purpose is to keep us safe and alive. Most of us will encounter experiences and circumstances when we feel unsafe, perhaps through worry or life stress. So, the mind will step in and try to find a solution using all the resources it knows. The mind is always looking for danger, be it some imagined crisis in the future or the neighbor's lawn mower. If the mind is always looking out for potential problems, then we can begin to identify and recognize the mind/brain's patterns.

Even when there are no problems, the mind will search through its files to create one. We all have experienced how the mind goes round and round even when everything is lovely and safe. We can be in the perfect moment, sitting in a beautiful setting, and the mind is thinking about any number of things it needs to figure out, stuff it needs to do, stuff that happened yesterday or last year, and the problems with other people. The mind looks for problems to solve because that's its job. The mind is a hyper-problem-solver and an extension of the subconscious brain. And getting curious about this is how we open the door to the unconscious realm, which influences us way more than we realize.

The mind can get very agitated when it imagines specific outcomes, yet nothing works. The mind is only aware of its reality, and it functions within this reality's "rules." Many rules to the mind's reality are programmed, so stepping beyond these rules can cause the brain to perceive danger. We can expect this along the journey when the mind can't predict an outcome. Awareness will naturally open to the Unknown, beyond the mind, as consciousness awakens from the separate self. We are the consciousness opening to its boundless nature, and the mind simply can't get on board for a while. It's still being influenced by its lower tendencies, which are the known. It is accustomed to having a plan and is now losing its capacity to predict outcomes. The old linear way of thinking belongs to the known, and the known is becoming less real and less reliable. Linear thinking also operates in time, and the sense of time begins to collapse, rendering this moment the only place to truly exist. When time begins to lose its reality, the mind of the separate self can get confused and frustrated. This is an in-between state of the mind, when we are leaving the old linear way of thinking and allowing a new way to emerge.

When the mind of the separate self cannot see an outcome, there is no life for "itself." It cannot see a future, so initially, things can look hopeless to the mind. This is very natural and very common. The mind's old way of operating is being dismantled. We may experience despair, where the mind asks, "What's the point?" or "Why bother with all this spiritual stuff? It's not working." Well, the truth is, it isn't working for a separate self. It is beneficial to be aware of this kind of mental tendency if it shows up, as it is so common. As we lean into the Unknown, with the mind losing its capacity to figure things out, it might turn around and try to grab onto anything it knows–people, places, and things. It most likely will.

Because the mind cannot see an outcome or a future, in rare cases, it might entertain thoughts of ending "its" life. The mind is turning on itself simply because it sees no other "solution." It cannot think outside of its reality; it only thinks, "If there is no future, there is no life, so I might as well end this one." This kind of thinking is the worst kind to the mind, and it can become a desperate entanglement of the mind thinking about its thinking. Perhaps some folks who end their own life were not suffering from "mental disease" (although, on some level, everyone does) but were experiencing an evolving consciousness, and the mind couldn't adapt. And the mind couldn't adapt because it did not know what was happening to its reality. It didn't understand this process. I sincerely hope this book helps those of you who encounter these tendencies, as I have.

I watched my mind have suicidal thoughts for a while and the intense feelings of terror that accompanied them. Fortunately, I could see what was causing these thoughts and remain present. Understanding this process is extremely important, and I am so grateful to Amma for this understanding. Without it, I don't know if I could have opened as much as I have, and this is the truth. A guide is priceless when we encounter these places that could potentially hang our process up. But there are no guarantees; some go all the way, and some won't. How and where consciousness opens is a mystery.

When awakened consciousness within the mind recognizes the old programs that need outcomes, it begins to let go. We identify how we have been striving for fulfillment, safety, and security through linear thinking and mental constructs. As consciousness awakens within the mind, we stop seeing the world through such a limited lens and begin to sense something different. We begin to sense that there is much more to learn, see, and realize.

At times, you might begin to feel the presence of consciousness within the interior of your brain, illuminating from within the infinite nature of existence. It feels good to have your brain filled with Presence. Allow your mind to witness this. Be the light that shows the mind the truth of what is unfolding within the mind-body. Be the mother (Awareness) who takes the child (mind) by the hand and shows the child that there are no problems to solve, no boogie men in the closet, and that it can relax. Be the infinite Love that shows the mind that all is well and it's not alone. Be patient with this child-mind. If we fight the mind in any way, it will not relax. You are the consciousness that illuminates the mind to awaken. You, as consciousness, will awaken within your mind. I invite you to feel yourself as the light showing the mind the truth, not in a thinking way, but in a direct, illuminating way. Let the mind witness all this. Stay conscious of this happening, and the mind will relax and let go of its need to know in a much gentler way. There is no need to prove to the mind that it is wrong; just allow the mind to witness itself so that it can relax.

The mind, an extension of the brain's neurological programs, only tries to keep the body safe. I know I repeated myself, but this is what the mind does—until it begins to awaken. As Awareness of the mind's tendencies increases, consciousness starts to liberate itself from the limited bondage of the mind. The tendencies of bondage must become conscious so that they become infused with consciousness. Tendencies, or habituated thoughts, create identification with the mind-body complex, while becoming conscious of them begins to

liberate this identification. The source of the mind is pure, unconditioned consciousness, so we must infuse the mind with its source.
It's like pouring fresh water into a glass of salt water; soon, the water
becomes clear and pleasant to drink.

Purification of the mind is essential if we want to harness its innate
power. The power of thought is the power of creation. This is why we
experience what we think through our feelings and perceptions in
daily life. When the mind is pure, as Source consciousness, we can
learn to harness the thought power to create something new. We can
learn to think and feel a new reality. These new experiences can alter
the brain's perceptions of danger into safety and inspiration. In this
way, all the programs from the past can be transformed.

We can influence the brain by experiencing more exalted feelings
like freedom and joy. When the brain feels these new feelings, it feels
safe. The absence of danger perceptions quiets the mind, and the
nervous system relaxes into something sublime. Allowing our experiences goes deeper into Source; allowing becomes a vehicle for the
experience of consciousness. Through the nervous system, we start to
make contact with the true Self. The brain witnesses this connection,
further convincing it of safety and well-being. Relaxation deepens,
and immense power informs the system of a new paradigm, one that
is free of limitation.

The mind is a fantastic tool, and a clear and open mind is a way
that consciousness can attract other possibilities. When we begin to
recognize that we have been living within a limited paradigm, due to
the thoughts that created them, we can begin to change. But deep
change comes from an intention free of the need to feel safe. This
intention is free from lack and dissatisfaction. We learn to work from
a free and open mind, free of the old linear way of thinking. Pure
Awareness dictates these thoughts, and they have a different type of

energy to them. They are pure creativity and potential. We are in the Unknown, where there is no linear thought. And when we are in the Unknown, we are open because being open is being in the Unknown.

The mind is a crucial part of this process of evolution, and when the mind is conscious and clear, our system is freed up to experience something new. We are fully present when the mind lets go of its need to know. The gate is open. This moment begins to reveal its depth and multi-dimensional nature. The mind also witnesses this, and the ceasing of old programs becomes more complete. This is another way of dissolving the separate self, the narrow and unconscious mind. It is another way that our limited ways of feeling and thinking evolve.

The folks in Quantum Physics have been doing many crazy experiments with the mind, showing us that when the conditioned mind is not in the picture, the door is open for anything to happen, possibilities that we may never have even considered. These experiments show us that the reality we know from our learned past is not the only reality. They show us that anything can happen if "the observer" (the conditioned mind) is absent. Everything is already happening, yet because we are all operating from a learned program, we can't possibly experience this phenomena. The conditioned mind blocks it. The conditioned mind believes in its reality without any other means to change it. We remain in a reality of pre-set rules, and our rules vary from person to person. We share standard rules, and others are variable, so we all are experiencing a different reality. Once the separate self is absent, all possibilities become available because the rules are absent, just like in the Quantum Physics experiments. The body-mind becomes something different, with the means to access possibility by tuning into energy and frequency. Possibility happens through the body-mind; it is used as an entry point for consciousness to explore its infinite nature. To stay open to this, to sense in your being that this is possible through you as a portal, is to remain open. Remember, your "you" is fading away for the gate to open. This is the process; the "you" can't get through the gate. What remains in your absence is the gate.

When Jesus spoke of entering heaven, he mentioned that a rich man could not enter God's kingdom; it would be easier for a camel to go through the eye of a needle. When we have many beliefs, opinions, and ideas that the separate self identifies with, our ego becomes "rich." Of course, a camel cannot enter the eye of a needle; it is entirely impossible. This is what our conditioned mind would say. Yet when Jesus speaks of this, he entertains its possibility. The beliefs, opinions, and ideas cannot enter, so if they are absent, can the unimaginable occur?

And what is the "eye of the needle"? Is it the tiny dot at the center of the Sri Yantra? Is accessing this tiny gate the actual opening of that gate, thereby allowing other possibilities to arise? Is this multidimensional reality God's Kingdom or Heaven on Earth? There is mention of the "Eye of the Needle" in many ancient religions, which all have a mystical facet:

- *Judaism: The Holy One said, open for me a door as big as a needle's eye, and I will open for you a door through which may enter tents and [camels?].*

- *Islam: To those who reject our signs and treat them with arrogance, no opening will there be of the gates of heaven, nor will they enter the garden, until the camel can pass through the eye of the needle*

- *Baha'i Faith: Present my best greetings to the honorable and spiritual women, to those who are very much attracted toward God, and particularly to that one who has proved that it is possible for a camel to pass through a needle's eye.*

We are here to know heaven on earth, and the dissolving of the separate self is the passage. We are the consciousness evolving from identification as a separate self to realizing our profound connection with all creation and beyond. The individual mind is not something to get rid of; instead, it gives us the means to see our limited reality and the clues we need to evolve from it. Like mud, the mind's limited way of seeing reality is the fertilizer. And from this fecund matter grows the lotus flower.

We are leaving behind an old paradigm, the only one we've known, and the new one has not yet revealed itself. Yet we stay in this place of in-between, for this is the place of maturation, where the seed of our eternal nature incubates and nourishes itself. Be patient; let yourself rest here. Allow the wisdom of all creation to reveal the wonder of a new Life within your being. This new Life is the eternal, Infinite Self that knows the way.

13.
Friction and Dissolution

There is an invisible strength within us;
when it recognizes two opposing objects of desire,
it grows stronger.

~Rumi

Have you ever had days when you woke up and discovered that you felt agitated for no reason? You feel edgy and tense and have no idea why: There's sand under your skin, and you feel like the world is one continuous test of your patience. Then, maybe you think something is wrong with you because you often feel this way. Welcome to Friction.

The word *Tapas* is a Sanskrit term meaning heat. It refers to the heat generated by two opposites rubbing against each other. Tapas can also mean hardship or austerity. Many great realized sages performed great austerities to go beyond the likes and dislikes of their mind. In this context, Tapas refers to two opposites rubbing against each other.

I experienced constant tension and friction within myself for many years- especially in the early years. This tension would be felt so often that I wondered if it would ever disappear. I would feel edgy, and I could sense a feeling of dissatisfaction within my being – like something wasn't quite right with my life. I had no idea where it was coming from for a long time, but fortunately, I had the wisdom to know that it meant I had more work to do. I would feel a tension that wouldn't subside for many days on end, and this took place even after I experienced significant shifts in consciousness. These days, friction occasionally appears in my body, but only now do I know its source. When friction is present, I know some illusions are being burned away.

Tapas, or friction, is the action of two opposites rubbing against each other. If they are honest, most people will admit that they often experience a slight tension just under the surface. They might experience a lot of tension or anything in between. Even though everything might be okay, they can still feel tension.

Friction or tension results from a conscious or unconscious belief rubbing up against what is happening or what we interpret as happening. So, if you believe your life *should* look like something, and if it isn't what it *should* be, you will experience friction. We've all experienced this. Maybe we call it stress, but if we take it a little deeper, all tensions have their genesis in a belief.

Tensions can be a powerful indicator that there might be a belief in your system rooted in ignorance. It can be a blessing in disguise because sometimes it can be difficult to see our beliefs in everyday life. Most beliefs are hidden in the unconscious, and when they emerge subconsciously, the brain may perceive them as dangerous and create a feeling of tension in the nervous system. It's like an alarm, saying danger! And this alarm goes off, and we look for the danger. But unfortunately, if we are still identified with the 3-D world, we will look outside ourselves for the danger. But the danger is within us.

When unconscious beliefs create tension, and we begin to get curious about this, we can learn to cooperate with the energy behind it. Life creates tapas, or opposites, so that we can recognize these hidden beliefs. As you become aware of the friction in your system, you can identify your, perhaps, subtle and oppositional belief systems. And because most of the subtle beliefs are simply programs from the past, we can begin to know them as energy rather than thought. If I have tension or friction, my brain is afraid of something. The programs from the past are neurological, so they will create a sensation in the system to warn us.

The thing about friction is that if we recognize a belief or warning signal by acknowledging that it is in us, we'll be okay. But if we keep thinking it's outside of us, we will look for ways to control the environment. And that rarely works if it's actual beliefs that are causing friction. But we may do this for a while, moving from here to there, changing relationships, friends, jobs, and houses. But the tensions follow us, and we need to take responsibility for them sooner or later. If we resist tensions to a great extent, the behavior can turn into emotional outbursts and projection.

We may also look for better experiences to change the tension. We may go on vacation or do other fun stuff. There is nothing wrong with that unless you're running away from yourself. Or we may look to spirituality for that special high that can come from meditation, singing bhajans, or even having a mystical experience. There is nothing wrong with these things either—I encourage them! But if we hope for some constant high to replace the tension, we are bypassing. We are repressing the neurological part of our being that is calling out for attention.

We might think that awakening or a spiritual experience will erase the tension. An awakening might make you feel better for a while, but many more beliefs will be seen after an awakening—so many more.

We must keep looking out for the drive to get a redeeming experience, an experience that is going to save us from our tension. Spiritual experiences don't save *us*, but they can inspire us. It is the light of consciousness that frees itself from beliefs. The light of consciousness, as Awareness, recognizes friction as a possible indicator of belief. So, even if you desire a redeeming spiritual experience, you could experience tension from not getting that experience. Desires can also be beliefs, so we might feel discontent and tension if a desire is not fulfilled. These desires fall under the category of likes and dislikes. All of this, in a nutshell, is what creates suffering.

If you believe that your life should be a certain way, and your life does not appear that way (to you), you may feel some tension under the surface. The tension might be very noticeable, or it might be something that you don't notice at all because the drive in you is so strong towards wanting the belief about your life to manifest perfectly. Tension is the result of how we interpret situations. If we interpret a situation or circumstance a certain way and we believe that that circumstance should be different, we will have tension. The tension results from the friction of the two opposites rubbing against each other–what you perceive versus what you believe.

All we need to do is notice that tension; we don't need to do anything else. We notice the tension, and then we become curious about it. We don't try to make the tension disappear by trying to be happy or telling ourselves that things will change soon and *then* we'll be satisfied. That is avoidance. Getting curious about the tensions in our system is the beginning of stopping the drive toward an imagined happy moment and seeing the beliefs you need to see. Or rather, see what's behind the drive for a better moment.

I have noticed that by simply being aware of friction in my system, I am allowing the heat of the *tapas* to dissolve belief systems that need to dissolve—sometimes without even being aware of what is being dissolved. So, you can now begin to perceive tension as a *good* thing. Of course, this isn't going to feel great at times; tension can be uncomfortable, yet if we know friction is dissolving what it needs to dissolve, we can develop a different attitude.

Knowing that old beliefs can dissolve when we feel tension is another doorway to allowing and surrender. It can also feel deeply satisfying in an odd way. Of course, we would rather be free of all tension. But I would choose the tension if I had to choose between tensions dissolving beliefs and no tensions with stagnant beliefs. Unconscious beliefs suck, honestly.

Knowing that my physiology is evolving as I feel tension allows me to stay open to tension. And because I experience tension, it doesn't mean that I am less evolved or still have a lot of stuff to work through. It simply means that the light of consciousness is doing what it came here to do: freeing the system of obsolete and limiting beliefs. This is why we are here in this life; tension is a small price for liberation from limiting beliefs.

The ancient Vedic teachings have many examples of ancient rishis, or sages, making great sacrifices to purify their minds. Old beliefs will arise when we go beyond modern society's comforts and live without much security. This is the point of entering caves or ashrams to purify the mind. Amma's ashram in India is a powerful purifier because it isn't all silent and serene as most would imagine an ashram would be. There is a lot of shakti, and there tends to be a lot of tapas. There are huge crowds that come to see Amma, along with many foreign tourists, so it doesn't fit the standard belief of a spiritual environment. It's a big melting pot of energy. I experienced many years of tension while living there in the early days, and this was back when the ashram was relatively small. But the energy of that place is incredibly effective at purifying the mind, as it is Amma's birthplace, and saturated with shakti. When I returned years later, I experienced it from a different perspective because all those earlier beliefs were absent. I found that quite interesting. But what I needed many years ago was perfect for me at that time. And now, it's perfect again.

The powerful thing about tension is that it has an effective way of changing our perceptions by dissolving the interpreter. When we perceive life without the interpreter, we see it as it is. Life becomes spontaneous and free without an interpreter because that is what it is naturally. When the interpreter is absent, we are not trying to find ourselves in what we perceive.

When we apply a belief to what we perceive, we are unconsciously trying to find ourselves in relation to what we see. This referencing type gives us a sense of security or comfort, but it is false. Even if what we interpret is negative and judgmental, it still gives us something to hold onto and is a false sense of comfort. If we walk around interpreting everything and everyone we perceive, we're not perceiving from a clear perspective. When we see life through the interpreter (the false, separate self), we create more density in our sense of separation.

Tension can be present when everything else seems to be okay. That is the beauty of the evolution of consciousness; it has its own intelligent and mysterious movement towards our inner illusions and fears. We do not have to do anything but stay open to tension; we are then giving consciousness permission to expose our beliefs. We allow it. Cooperating with how consciousness reveals illusions is in alignment with your evolutionary process. If you feel tension, you can be conscious enough to recognize that you want precisely what is happening. The deepest part of you wants this. If we think for a minute that we shouldn't be having tension, then we are creating a belief that opposes the intelligence of consciousness. Remember, enlightenment is our complete cooperation with the flow of consciousness and its tendency to expose beliefs. If we oppose our inner experience, we interpret it from a belief. When we cooperate, we realign and attune to the power of what's actually true. This power is the power of Light; the pure Light of Awareness.

The power of light is naturally attracted to anything that is not light. We may find ourselves in many seemingly dark places. But if we know what is true, those places will not seem dark unless the mind interprets them as dark. The places the Light is attracted to can feel like doorways to new freedom, but initially, they may feel tight. There may be tension. But it is this tension that is the doorway. The beliefs and perceptions that the Light shines upon are the means for the Light to know itself more fully. The dark becomes a beckoning to the Light, and the Light responds by lighting up the dark. This is the pivotal moment when we learn to allow tension or tightness—allowing means to align with the movement of Light into the darkness. Aligning with the infinite intelligence at work by allowing is how we begin to dismantle our ideas about tension and tightness. Only the mind's interpretation names tension as negative. As we mature, we start to see that each moment of tension has a huge blessing for opening the nervous system to the Infinite reality. Allowing ourselves to feel everything opens the door for the Light to come in.

You might sometimes feel the friction of tension in your body, and it might not feel so great. Your mind might interpret it as edgy or aggravated. Your brain might recoil from the feeling and create a story. See if you can allow the body to *feel tense* without believing it is wrong and that you must do something to eliminate it. See if you can objectify the tension by being aware that it is only a part of you. You are the Awareness of the tension. Objectifying removes the identification with the tension. The tension is merely something happening within the mind-body complex, and learning to accommodate it is an essential part of our evolution. Once you learn to acknowledge and allow the tension, the intelligence within will do the rest.

If the mind understands the function of friction and tension and can see its benefits, it will be much more open to tension in the future. There will be more tension, yet as we mature, we lose the identification with it. We are an evolving process of dissolving the separate self, and tensions will become familiar. Remember, friction and tension are just energy in a contracted form. The power of transformation is pure energy, or Shakti. It will blow through you and cause contractions as it clears away the obsolete programs. Without energy, we wouldn't change. This energy can't hurt you. But you must go through these processes to transform into a pure instrument for the Divine. Just remember, what is blowing through you is taking care of everything.

If we are looking for a comfortable, enlightened state, we will not be open to generating energy through accommodating friction; we will be in an unconscious drive towards feeling better. We will resist the experience of something new and unprecedented. The power of *tapas* can generate lots of energy, which means lots of friction to dissolve the separation conditioning in our system. Everyone will experience friction at some point in this process, and the more familiar we get with it, the more effective it can be.

Our physiology is designed to be a vessel for energy. As the system begins to experience its design as an open pipe, the dense identification with the body begins to fade. The brain becomes more conscious of the power of Shakti within, and as it witnesses the changes within the mind-body complex, it begins to perceive this energy as safe. Resistance to tensions is reduced and is seen as beneficial. Amma has often said there is so much Light available, but if we encountered it in our current state, we would get burnt up. The nervous system needs to be purified by the fire of Shakti to accommodate it. The fire of Shakti creates the friction that purifies.

If you're working on yourself and have developed some self-awareness, you might be more prone to friction. When we are aware of our inner perceptions and beliefs that may be outdated, Shakti comes in to purify. She knows when we are open enough and will move towards our unconscious programs to open us even more. And the more open we become, the purifying fire will go into pure existentialism. It will expose the deepest core of our separation, the fundamental belief that we are separate from all life.

There is no need to look for an ideal, comfortable, permanent experience because there isn't one. So, allow yourself to relax into any tension here right now. Our sense of stability will be found in the relaxation of what we are experiencing, not in its absence. This is also how we regulate the nervous system. When we cooperate with what our experience is, through allowing, we strengthen our alignment as the Supreme Self because this is where pure allowing originates. With this profound connection to our True Self, we grow more courageous to expose the roots of the separate self.

I have witnessed Amma experience intense friction in her body, especially in the old days in India. It would be so hot for her, and she would yell at everyone to stay away from her while giving Darshan. It seemed like her body was experiencing a tremendous amount of energy, yet it never seemed like it was a problem for her. She would keep giving Darshan in an incredibly loving way. Then, it would change, and she would be fine the next day. I don't see her going through those adjustments as much anymore, and she also doesn't seem as wild in her oneness with Goddess Kali. In the early days, she was on fire! Amma would be in over-the-top bliss during bhajans, losing herself completely, swaying and rocking vigorously from side to side. Nowadays, she seems to be at the same depths, but her body isn't so affected, so it doesn't appear as unusual. Amma's energy field seems vaster to me now; her body seems much more able to accommodate the immense presence within and the thousands of people that come to her. Of course, I do not know what is going on with Amma's body, as this is simply my mind's interpretation.

Our physical bodies are designed to accommodate the Infinite field on the physical plane. Our bodies can go through all kinds of crazy things at times. Some of these things might cause the brain to feel unsafe. Since the brain needs to feel safe and wants to keep the body safe, we might experience the effects of *fight or flight* during this process. Fight or flight is an acute stress response through which the brain prepares the body to survive a threat. Increased cortisol and adrenaline, high levels of physical tension, and insomnia can all be a part of a prolonged fight or flight experience. I didn't realize this was happening until much later in my journey. I had constant tension and sleeplessness. What my body has been through and how it has bounced back shows me the resiliency of the human nervous system. I can also see that a prolonged fight or flight response can dissolve much of the density of the separate self. I don't know if this is ideal, but it was the way for me.

Your physiology knows how to open, which may look different than everyone else's. Don't try to analyze your process, but rather deepen your relationship with the energy within, the energy that is freeing itself by opening the system. This relationship with the fire of Shakti, or Divine Light, is the most important relationship for you to have. It is your connection to the Divine on the most intimate level within your body. It knows just how to open the entire physiology to receive the Infinite. Your process has its own authentic way of unfolding. Don't copy anyone else, not even for a minute! Don't compare your process with others either, as that will weaken your relationship with the inner wisdom unfolding within you. Maintain the connection as it grows stronger while allowing the mind to witness and be part of it. This relationship with Shakti is the ultimate path of evolution, and the more complete our cooperation is with it, the deeper it will go.

14.
Chaos

When someone beats a rug, the blows are not against the rug but against the dust in it.

~Rumi

Amma's ashram in Kerala, India, has a magical presence within its walls. This is where she was born and began manifesting her extraordinary love and compassion to the world. Amma endured intense trials throughout childhood while expressing her devotion to the Supreme consciousness. Here at this ashram, many people from all over the world come to be close to Amma. Walking through the front gates, you can feel a soothing presence greeting you. This presence is highly transformative for those who stay and immerse themselves within its walls. The ashram is imbued with a heightened level of Shakti, so people can sometimes find themselves pushed to their limits.

I will share a story that happened to me while living at the Amritapuri Ashram. It was a challenging time, yet looking back, I recognize that what took place was exactly what was needed. The transformational power of Shakti works in very mysterious ways, and most of the time, this profound transformation happens on a level that we cannot recognize because the mind cannot comprehend the deep layers of its unconscious conditioning. My early years at the ashram were continuous periods of profound transformation. Because my mind could never understand how my purification process needed to be, I experienced times of deep confusion and disorientation. I did recognize, however, a power of deep intelligence and goodness at work, which continues to this day. I feel blessed to have Shakti's unconditional Love dismantle my conditioned mind's dysfunction. During those early years, every time my confusion became overwhelming, Amma was always there with her loving embrace and impeccable grace, constantly inspiring me to keep going.

The year is 1996, my third year at Amritapuri Ashram. I live in the "Krishna Dorm," a dormitory on the second floor of the main temple building. I am sharing the dorm with about 24 other women; many are visiting the ashram for an extended stay. My bunk is a lower bunk in the middle of the room under a fan; I need to be under the fan as much as possible because I suffer tremendously from the heat. My body is always hot from all my meditation and because of my body's natural constitution. My daily schedule includes getting up every morning at 4 am to take a bath and go down to the temple to take part in the morning Archana, the chanting of the thousand names of the Divine Mother. I never miss a morning of Archana; even if I feel ill, I force myself to get up. Because I get up so early, I must be in bed by 10 pm, and the dorm rules are lights out by 10 pm. I am the only woman out of the whole dorm that gets up every morning, and I am always surprised by this because I get so much out of the morning chanting. But I am very quiet every morning not to wake anyone up.

A German woman has recently moved into the dorm, but I am unfamiliar with her. She feels a little edgy, so I keep my distance. She is sleeping in a bunk two over from me. She has started staying up late and keeping the lights on, disturbing me as I need to get to sleep. She stays up till 10:30 or even 11 pm with the lights on. Sometimes I can fall asleep, but often I cannot, so when 4 am comes, I am very sleepy. I decided to say something to her when I saw her again.

The following day, after breakfast, I am alone in the dorm. Amma is scheduled to come to the temple and give Darshan, so most folks are out getting their chores done before Amma comes.

The German lady walks into the dorm—her name is Rita. She feels edgy again, and although I try to avoid anyone who feels "testy," I know I have to say something to her about the lights. Rita is not the easiest person to be around; she might be slightly unbalanced. But I am tired from being kept awake at night, and since I am the only one who gets up early, I am the one who needs to say something.

I decide this is the best time to talk to her, so I walk over to the wall where the rules are posted, and I calmly say to her, "Namah Shivaya?" (This is what we always say to each other whenever we want to get someone's attention, say hello, or ask them a question or any infinite number of different things). Rita glares at me as I calmly point out to her the rule that lights need to be out by 10 pm each night. I quickly mention that I need to get up early for Archana, and I can't sleep because she is keeping the lights on.

My words light Rita's fuse, and she blows up big time. She is tall and thin, taller than me, and I am relatively tall. She stalks over to me in a red-faced rage and starts shouting, "OH! Do you think you are in charge here? Who do you think you are? You think you are such a little princess and are always right? You don't own this ashram, you know! You don't make the rules! You are not in charge here!"

As she is screaming at me, she is getting closer and closer, and I can see that she is in the grip of some kind of fit, like she has tipped over mentally and is losing her grip on reality. She is right in front of me screaming, and suddenly, she pushes me hard, and I fall backward over a trunk that is on the floor behind me. I land on my back, and from nowhere, an Amma photo lands in my hands. Rita is standing over me, still screaming, and she starts to kick me as I lay there on the floor clutching the Amma photo.

Now, something very peculiar is happening inside me; I want Rita to keep kicking me; I want her to get all that rage out of her. It is the weirdest feeling, and I am not afraid in the least bit. I feel my whole being let go of controlling the situation and letting go of whatever wants to happen.

A woman named Padma enters the room and sees Rita standing over me, screaming like a lunatic. It must be evident to Padma what is happening, and she yells at Rita to stop. Padma demands to know what is happening, but Rita runs out of the room. Padma approaches me, where I am lying with the Amma photo, reaches down, and holds me. I shakily tell Padma how Rita went bonkers after I asked her to respect the lights-out rule. Padma asks me if I am hurt, and I am amazed to say that I am not, but I feel pretty shaken up. I look over to the windows, and I notice that there is a group of Indian women looking in at me. Padma says that when she came up the stairs and saw all the Indian women at the window, she knew something was happening inside the dorm. I am so relieved that Rita is gone that my inner protection drops, and I start to cry.

Suddenly, I feel like a nervous wreck and must leave the dorm. I need some space to breathe. Padma gives me her Amma doll to hold onto while I go sit up on the roof and try to calm down. I can't believe how shaken up I am, and I start to sense that Rita has unlocked some strange feelings in me that I had no idea were there.

After some time, I want to see Amma, so I go down from the roof to the inner temple. As I enter, I feel calmed a bit by the energy of the inner temple. A few people are waiting for Amma to come, so I sit on the women's side beside Amma's peetham. Very soon, Amma enters, bowing to everyone, sits down, and begins giving Darshan. Immediately, Amma looks at me with a questioning look that shows concern. But any intimate time with Amma is short-lived as right behind me sits another crazy woman, an Indian woman named Anima, who just delights in annoying everyone around her. She is directly behind me and starts to push against my back, and she laughs at me when I ask her to stop. There is plenty of room, so I don't understand why she is pushing on me, and within minutes, my tolerance for being touched reaches a breaking point. I start to cry because I simply cannot sit there anymore, and I need to be with Amma. Amma is still looking at me with great concern. But I can't stay; I must get away from here. I get up, and as I walk towards the back door, I cry, and Amma's eyes follow me. As I walk out, I hear Amma yelling at the crazy woman, Anima, to get up and leave; she is not allowed to sit near Amma anymore. I hear Anima start to whine and beg Amma, but Amma is shouting angrily, and I feel a little better that Anima is getting scolded by Amma. I am so shaken up that I go back to the roof and cry.

A little later, I go to the western office and tell the woman in charge there what had happened in the Krishna dorm. She listens attentively, then compassionately, and tells me I should tell Amma what happened. But I don't want to go down there amongst all the people. There is so much tension in my body, and the thought of being touched, even accidentally, feels like too much. The woman understands and gives me a different room to stay in. She says she will talk to crazy Rita and decide what to do with her. So, I pack up all my stuff, which takes me the rest of the afternoon. At least it gives me something to do while my body tries to calm down.

For the next few days, I still feel very shaky, and whenever I see Rita, I get a panicky feeling in my system. It's weird because she didn't hurt me at all; there weren't even any bruises from where she kicked me. I feel traumatized, and I can't get over it. I need to see Amma.

I write a short note to Amma that I have translated into Malayalam so Amma can read it herself. I do not want to make a scene, but I need to talk to her about what I am going through and ask her to help me calm down. As I go up to Amma for my Darshan, one of her attendants takes my note and reads it boldly out loud. Oh, god, there go my plans for discretion. Amma holds me for a while, rubbing my back, which feels like a healing balm for my nerves. Then Amma lifts me, looks compassionately into my eyes, and says (translated), "Amma knows what you are going through; she too used to get beaten for no reason."

I get up from my Darshan, feeling that a huge weight has been lifted, but not entirely. I still feel traumatized, but now Amma knows and is part of my experience. Amma has just shared her trials with me and related them to what I have gone through. When Amma was a young girl, she was beaten regularly by her mother and by other relatives for no reason. Yet she always knew that it was part of her Dharma and God's will, and these trials were to make her stronger. When Rita assaulted me, I had the same strange feeling that it was supposed to happen, and an inner intelligence wanted it to happen.

After Darshan, I feel much better, but I am still panicky whenever I see Rita, and she looks pretty bad herself. What kind of karmic ride are we on here?

I have decided to go on the North India tour. Even though I know it could be challenging, the joys of being on the road with Amma are worth any discomfort. I need to be in her presence as I am still feeling somewhat traumatized. Nothing is relieving these shaky feelings, so if anything can change them, the North India tour can!

But as soon as we reach our first stop, I see that Rita has been allowed to join us. And a few cities later, she is in the same room as I am! I feel so irritated that she is here that I don't consider anything but myself and my discomfort. My self-absorbed attitude only perpetuates my feelings of shakiness. I don't notice that I have created a new story for myself, but we are on tour, and anything can happen.

We are at a new stop and are staying at a hermitage. There is an open space with several areas separated by walls but open to the outside. We all sleep on mats on the floor, side by side. Looking over the grounds below, I have a nice spot by the edge. Over on the far side of the open space are four shower stalls, and about 75 women share these. The shower is a bucket bath; we must first fill our buckets outside the stalls. Sometimes, getting all our laundry done can take a while, as we all must wait our turn for the shower stalls and the buckets.

I am waiting in line for a shower with my bucket of water. I have been waiting a bit, but I am next in line. The door opens to the stall in front of me. The girl gets out, and I get ready to step in and take my shower. Suddenly, from my left, the crazy Indian woman Anima steps in front of me and enters the shower stall! She is standing there proudly, proclaiming that she will take a shower. I am stunned that she would do something so selfish and rude. But I don't react at all. I feel a strong, quiet presence inside me as I ask her, "Oh, you're going to take a shower now, are you?"

"Yes," she says with a crazy grin, "I am going to shower now!" She is proud of herself for this act.

I feel myself reach for my bucket, which is by my side and full to the top with water. I asked her again, and she once more declares that she will shower now.

I take the bucket, and with sudden superwoman strength, I swing it back and dump the whole bucket of water over Anima's head. She's still wearing her sari. She looks at me with absolute shock, and all around me, I can feel a stunned silence as others witness this episode.

Anima runs out of the shower stall, crying. I go and refill my bucket, calmly enter the stall, and take my shower. I can hear the Indian girls whispering in Malayalam, and I am sure they are all just as shocked as I am about what I did. As I shower, I feel detached from what anyone out there is thinking about me. I simply cannot care any longer. When I leave the shower stall, I feel dozens of eyes watching me, some with amusement and some with condemnation.

I return to my sleeping mat and start getting ready for the program. I am nervous and shaking all over. I can't believe I lost control like that, but it felt like some other force picked that bucket up and poured the water over Anima's head. Did I do that? It is entirely out of my character, even though Anima has been driving me and many others nuts for far too long.

Uh-oh, here comes the woman in charge of the Western women on the tour. I know she knows what I did. I don't feel like dealing with this; I just want this mess to disappear! The woman sits down and tells me what she has heard from the others about the bucket of water over Anima's head. Is there anything I want to add to this story?

I start to crack, I mean really crack. All the tension from the past weeks comes rushing up to the surface, and I start to sob. I tell the woman I am sorry and feel bad, but I just couldn't stop myself! The woman seems a bit taken aback by the energy of my emotions; she tells me she understands, but I still need to go and apologize to Anima. Aargh. So, I go and find Anima on her mat. She is now in a dry sari, but her friend steps in between us as I approach Anima.

"You have a face like a flower, but you're like a monster inside!" she says.

Great. I look at Anima, and we both start crying. I tell her I am sorry, and she rushes to me, hugs me, and tells me she is too. We stand there and hug while all these Indian women around us are whispering, and I don't understand what they are saying. Nor do I care. I have been through so much these past weeks and am so done caring about what anyone thinks about me. I know that some of these women are judging me, even though they all know that Anima misbehaves most of the time. But now, Anima is as soft as a teddy bear and feels vulnerable and tender.

After that stop, something begins to feel different. I feel lighter and don't care much about what others think, which is unusual for me. I usually would be very concerned about what others thought about me. Rita is still around, but I don't care what she thinks about me either; yet, I am more aware of the pain of her previous behavior. I also feel free of the panicky feelings that seeing her used to evoke. I feel more connected to myself, as if a new self-respect and sense of worth are emerging.

The incredible thing is that Anima is acting entirely differently. She is sitting with Amma very peacefully now, smiling and giving up her seat so others can sit down—something she would never have done before. She is meditating for long periods with her eyes closed, and she doesn't seem interested in pushing her way to be close to Amma. The transformation is astonishing.

I know that something quite miraculous has happened in all this messy business. This entire process has been like a dream, and now I am beginning to wake up. I am waking up to a world where people are kind and genuine to one another. There seems to be a new respect from some Indian women towards me, as if they, too, notice that something quite magical has happened. All I know is that I have been on a wild ride, and I am glad the ride is over- for now.

15.
Complete Surrender

Offering yourself into the burning yajna-kund (sacred fire) of the infinite power of God–that is real seva.

Atma-samarpanam–offering yourself–is a law of the Universe. A few rare individuals live according to this Truth.

~Mata Amritanandamayi

In this moment, right here, right now, lives everything whole and complete. Just as it is, this moment is the only place to find your True Self, the Atman. This moment, just as it is, invites you to know what is True in on a deep level within your being, and this moment will only reveal this when we surrender entirely to our Self, our True Self.

Surrender is a word that doesn't sit well with some folks. For those who resist this word, I invite you to question your ideas about surrender. You cannot know what surrender is unless you are traveling the path of surrender. Unless you have experienced the Grace that a complete surrender attracts, the concept of surrender might appear quite unfortunate. You may feel it to be threatening. But for those of us who know the power of surrender, surrender is the name of the game.

An invitation to surrender is an opportunity to get completely real with ourselves, deep down. It is the means to see where our grasping is—where we still are making our demands in Life, and interpreting life through the lens of the separate self. Surrender is the vehicle to relinquish the separate self once and for all. It is the cleanest and most effective way to dissolve the ignorance within the nervous system, revealing pure Cosmic consciousness.

Surrender and devotion are synonymous. When we begin to see the power of the Divine behind everything, we naturally let go to it. When we genuinely long to be a vessel for the Infinite, we must surrender to the infinite power because only this power knows how to design a vessel for itself.

When we are devoted to the Infinite, we align ourselves to a different life than we were living previously. The separate self is living from "my will." In surrender, we become conscious and aligned with "thy will." When we are aligned with "thy will," our relationship with the Divine becomes unconditional. We begin to trust most profoundly that everything happening is for our own benefit. We stop making demands, and we begin tuning into Life. We begin sensing its intelligence, allowing it to inform our system.

We are not surrendering our experiences or circumstances so that they will improve. We are not surrendering to be saved. When we have surrendered completely, we have lost the capacity to even consider the outcome of the surrender. We are empty of any personal agenda, so we are completely in the Unknown.

When we are in complete surrender, we are present. We are here with this moment in its entirety. We feel the invitation to surrender intuitively, which is happening internally. We are surrendering how we relate to this moment. We may feel angry, sad, or awkward about this moment, but we offer all of this to the Divine to be transformed.

It may change, or it may not. But this infusion of consciousness that happens through surrender makes surrender so powerful.

The more mature consciousness is in the body, the more sensitive we become to these invitations. We become more sensitive to surrender as energy within the body. Surrender is a feeling–maybe a strong feeling–as consciousness awakens from any grasping in the nervous system. The invitation to surrender will become increasingly more subtle as consciousness matures, with the openings in our system becoming increasingly more spacious and noticeable.

Whenever we truly allow ourselves to have an experience, the experience of this moment as we feel it in our bodies, we surrender by allowing it to be. There is an absence of a drive towards any other experience than the one that is happening, the real one, deep at our core. We do not have any beliefs about the experience–no thoughts wishing for it to go away or blaming it on something. We are completely present and open–no matter what is happening within us. We can have all kinds of human-like feelings or fears, but who is to say they are wrong? Surrender allows us to see that our humanity is a means for consciousness to know itself. Our limited and habitual understanding relinquishes control to something beyond our comprehension.

Consciousness is everything we experience; only the separate self has created the belief that this is untrue, and we cannot realize this without surrender.

When we surrender, it is the separate self that is surrendered, along with any ideas that it has about this moment. We then can be open to any experience hiding under the surface, the ones that have been unconsciously avoided. When the separate self begins to dissolve, we lose the filters managing the unconscious undesirable emotions. Most folks have potent filters, and when an emotional charge is triggered, they will do anything to eliminate their experience of it. These managing strategies will become more subtle and tricky the deeper we go.

When the filters come down, the dissolution of separation can feel out of control as intense emotions rush to the surface. We will all experience the loss of filters differently. It is important to have emotional intelligence before the filters come down; otherwise, things can get messy. But then again, messiness might also be part of the plan, which can dissolve the illusions of control of the separate self.

It's common for folks who have had a shift in consciousness to do spiritual bypassing. *Spiritual bypassing* is the avoidance of unresolved darker feelings. After knowing expansiveness, they don't want to feel the darker feelings within. These heavy feelings don't match their ideas of awakening, and a type of dismissal happens. But what these folks are dismissing are the means consciousness uses to open the nervous system and keep this evolutionary process unfolding. They are missing the essential point of evolution: opening the nervous system enough to access our unlimited potential. Surrendering through our experience is a powerful way to see if we are holding onto the old paradigm of the separate self. In deep surrender, we will see everything, every remnant of the illusion of "my life." All forms of control, managing, and strategies need to be removed.

I've noticed that the current neo-Advaita teachings that are popular in the West (they began in the early 1990s) promote spiritual-bypassing and mental dismissal. They do not teach the basic preparatory steps needed to develop self-awareness. We need to have a strong practice of self-awareness to see through ignorance. Otherwise, any intellectual application may be dangerous. We can get trapped in a false realm of delusion for a long time. Only the separate self wants to bypass. This is my observation, and I am grateful to have a Master who has pointed out any tendency in myself to bypass. Because we all have these tendencies, and if we aren't aware of them, we're lost. Bypassing does no one any good, and people can "dry up" and stagnate in their growth. Bypassing doesn't allow surrender to go deep into the nervous system. The opportunity to evolve significantly diminishes as spiritual bypassing becomes a learned, hard-wired program in the brain. Bypassing becomes a way of life.

Surrender is not something we learn how to do. It is far better to admit you don't know how to surrender. When we realize this truth deep in the nervous system, we relinquish any conceptual understanding of what surrender must look like. Surrender is not a plan that you can foresee. It does not mean that we need to let go of "things" in our life, such as our job, spouse, or money, although that could happen.

Usually, it takes many years of small surrenders before we are mature enough to let go of ourselves completely. Our physiology needs a gradual rewiring to accommodate all the energy available when it is emptied of lifetimes of beliefs, hopes, identifications, attachments, fears, and insecurities. Illusion is an entangled package, and the deeper we go into surrender, the more we see how entangled it is within us. This entanglement is called Maya, the grand Illusion, and this is what is being surrendered. Maya is how we perceive and experience this three-dimensional existence that we live in. It is the projection of beliefs onto our internal and external world. When we become aware that we are caught in Maya's net and do not see things as they are, we awaken as consciousness. We sense that there is more to see and are curious. Many folks feel entangled, yet they are not ready to be curious. We need to recognize entanglement in our individual lives so that we begin to investigate. We must see that we are entangled in order to surrender to break free of the net. But we will cling to the net; you can count on it. This is our only reality, so clinging and grasping are natural. We cannot understand what is beyond, but slowly, as our systems open, we will have the capacity to let go and be free.

Honesty is necessary to realize how deep the insecurities of the separate self are in our system. Every time we experience grasping and resistance, fear and insecurity, there is an invitation to surrender. As consciousness matures, its capacity to recognize internal insecurities increases. Internal insecurities are aspects of the separate self that may be completely hidden. The separate self can even hide in pseudo-surrender, telling itself that it has surrendered while obscuring its grasping and insecurities. But that won't work for long because the separate self can't surrender; it can't surrender itself because it IS its grasping and insecurity. Only the unconditioned Awareness can truly surrender, as it lets go of the need to believe in any more control mechanisms that make up the separate self.

I was introduced to the meaning of surrender when I went back and forth to India. I would work in the West and get enough money to spend about eight months a year with Amma. My longing to be with Amma made it imperative that I return to India every year during this period. The crazy gotta-get-there-or-die feeling began after my first meeting with her in 1993 and lasted for nine years. And because I wanted to stay each year in India for as long as I could, I would wait until my money was gone before returning to the West. I would save enough for the bus fare from Denver to the western part of Colorado, with a little bit left for food. Each time I returned to the West, I would have no money, job, car, house, or family in the area to call upon for help.

I had no clue what I would do or where I would go when I got off the plane in Denver. Sometimes, I would sleep in the airport until I could figure out what came next. I found places to sleep in basements, cars, storage lockers, tents, and on the couches of people who didn't want me there. It was an extremely challenging nine years, and if that desperate drive hadn't been there, I could never have done it. Something took over my life for that period, forcing me to surrender every idea about how "I" thought things should be. As a result, I lost several old friends; these friends thought I should have it more "together." That was quite painful. But those friends had no idea what was driving me to live the life I was living. I had no idea, either! There was no way I could explain what was happening. Sometimes, I would move to another town entirely, changing jobs because of certain difficult situations. I've lived in shacks with mice running all over me while I slept, with no heat or electricity, hauling laundry on a bicycle in the rain, and so much more. It was a tremendous sacrifice, but I was so driven that it didn't feel like a sacrifice. There was only Love, and that is what was driving everything.

When I was in the West, I felt very isolated and alone. How could anyone understand what I was going through? This fed into my core story of not being understood, which I was unaware of at the time. Yet I remember those years with gratitude, for they were so deep and rich; it was a time of pure devotion to my process and my love of Amma. And so much was let go of…because this was the only thing I could do.

If I had my choice, I would wish it had been a little more secure and comfortable, but I didn't have a choice: the whole drama was unfolding just as it was. How my situations presented themselves left me with little option but to let go, again and again. It was a perfect set-up. I lived on the edge of not knowing and intuited that this was how it was meant to be. Any thoughts or beliefs that resisted the conditions, and there were many, had to be let go of; otherwise, I would have gone nuts. The surrender process beckoned me to open to the Presence I sensed around me and within me. It felt like my Beloved, my Amma, and a blissful opening to her. Presence became my companion through many hardships; She became the balm for my grieving heart when all else seemed hopeless.

When I was in the States, I felt lost. There didn't seem to be a place for me here anymore. In Amritapuri Ashram, I was only a visitor, so I didn't have the same privileges as the residents. I remember times when I would have to share a room with tourists who used to stop by the ashram for a night or two. They were nice enough, but I felt so disconnected with worldly pursuits during that time that it only added to my sense of isolation and feelings of being misunderstood. I felt as if I had no home anywhere–no place to lay my head. And I desperately wanted some semblance of security! But I was in free-fall.

I began to feel the surrender process deep in my body, in my nervous system. Because I had the physical form of Amma in my life, she became the presence that supported my process of letting go. Amma's presence strengthened me as I opened up to her and let go of *everything*. Again and again, deeper and deeper, I felt my being let go. I somehow knew this was the process, even though I didn't like it at all. I made no demands on Amma and never approached her to ask for advice or help. The only time I ever approached her about my challenges became a fiasco, which I will relate to in the next chapter.

The deeper the surrender of the separate self, the more present we are. There is less in the way of our communion with this moment. When we connect with the presence of Now, our nervous system will naturally open to it. Surrender allows us to feel deeply the beauty that is the essence of NOW–a beauty to be received through our open systems. We sense the pure goodness of our Beloved Presence, and our system knows it is here to support us. It is our best friend, and our system can begin to relax through this friendship. We become increasingly more sensitive to our beloved friend as we open to receiving the subtle transmissions offered. This is Grace. These are the silent transmissions, and the system can open to a new way of knowing through silence. Our system is informed of its true essence and connection to the Totality. It begins to lose the capacity to react to the world as a separate, insecure self. The nervous system relaxes into surrender as a natural abiding resting place. It is aligned with the inevitable, or "thy will."

When we are aligned with the presence of NOW, when the nervous system completely cooperates with the inevitable, we are emptied of attachments. At this moment, we are not attached to beliefs or hopes. At this moment, our mind can be shown its inherent emptiness, that its true nature is empty of these attachments. It has been these attachments that have given us the illusion of separation. Allowing the mind to witness its emptiness means recognizing the absence of a separate self. Let your mind keep seeing its empty nature, and the nothing that is everything will bloom in your mind and shift its perception of the world.

Surrender is entirely organic. If we stay open to life, we will see within what we need to see, which may be in opposition to this moment. When we are open, we have an inner, deep knowing of how to let go. If we are unafraid of surrender, letting go can release potent energy. The surrender process is a driving force that will tear down our walls of illusion, revealing an unbelievable richness under the surface.

Surrender is the fertilizer for our hearts to bloom fully. It strengthens Love within the Heart as it keeps opening to the Unknown. The Heart's intelligence recognizes itself as the Unknown, beyond the mind's comprehension. This level of pure Love is unconditional because the will of the separate self is absent. Complete surrender is the absence of a separate self. We are all discovering what this means for us in our own lives. We will know each invitation to surrender when it is upon us and not before. It is such a beautiful process, although it can sometimes be scary. But we feel the Heart's guidance, and then, one day, we recognize that surrender has become a pure flow of Life. Letting go has matured into complete surrender.

Any idea that we will "get" something from surrender won't last when we give ourselves to the Beloved Presence. The Love of the Beloved is fierce and unconditional and will expose all our agendas. Love will expose everything that is not of itself, as it only wants to experience itself. With self-awareness, we can see all the agendas of the separate self. And in that seeing, we will have the opportunity to let it go when we are ready.

Surrender allows us to get in touch with that part of ourselves that must know the other side of surrender. It will enable us to feel the essence that exposes all illusions within our being. Over time, it allows us to recognize a power within that keeps going and isn't lessened by trials and hardships. True surrender pulls out the strength within our being, which moves beyond all fears. Surrender allows us to recognize that "Thy will" has been driving this vessel all along, and as a result, the old paradigm of "my will" fades away. We feel lighter, and the intelligence within begins to lead with unwavering conviction.

When fully surrendered, we are set up for success because we are fully present with what is relevant right now. We are not concerned about anything else. The Beloved is guiding us from within. This is the only place we want to be.

We are designed to be entirely authentic vessels, and not meant to copy anyone. Only the inner Self knows the design inherent in the body and will keep revealing all the inner workings, guiding life beyond anything previously known. We stay relevant, and this is how authenticity is born.

Over the decades of being with Amma, I have been extremely fortunate to witness her expressions of Divine Love. She could be sweet and compassionate one moment and show a terrifying fierceness in the next. She is constantly being moved by what is relevant to the moment. Witnessing this diversity has allowed me to drop my ideas about what spiritual enlightenment should look like. We are all uniquely wired systems, and if we can stay open to our system's intelligence, we can evolve beyond ourselves.

In a moment of surrender, the separate self can feel much fear and confusion; surrender doesn't imply that we are not bothered or that the process should be easy. Surrendering can sometimes be extremely challenging simply because we don't know where we are headed. Remember, we are the awareness of confusion and fear. Be curious about what fear is saying and what it hopes for. Fear can be a powerful energy that opens the system, so you might as well use it. We can't possibly know what the future might bring, and the deeper we go, the more we lose the capacity to imagine a future. Naturally, the unconscious programs might get triggered about that. We must have patience in this process, as it takes many years to reach a place of complete surrender. But looking back, we can see how our system gradually adjusts to the process.

Take the time to sit in silent meditation, immerse your being in the stillness of this moment, and recognize the available loving support. Let your spirit be nurtured

and cared for. This process does not have to be difficult, although it may be challenging. Allow the system to open to what is true right here and right now. Surrender aligns consciousness with our experience so that our being can know absolute communion with the Totality. Doubt cannot survive in complete surrender. It will vanish, along with the separate self. Surrender opens the portal, revealing the presence of the True Self as the Totality.

16.
Death by Microphone

Thunder is good, thunder is impressive;
But it is Lightning that does the work.

~MARK TWAIN

I am sitting with the rest of the Ashram residents in the temple hall, wait-ing for Amma to come out. It's Tuesday, when the residents spend the day with Amma, and the ashram is closed to public Darshan. We will spend the day meditating with Amma, asking her questions and sharing in the Prasad lunch (food that has been blessed). It's the best day of the week.

I am sitting about halfway back on the floor. This is where I usually sit, as I have plenty of room, yet I am close enough to Amma to see her eyes and know when she is looking at me. I usually like to sit a little bit away from Amma as I find the energy beside her a little intense. It's like being close to a furnace, and I am hot enough.

The year is 1999, so I've spent most of the last six years at Amritapuri, only leaving when I run out of money. I have been increasingly bothered by the way my life is going. I have seen so many new Westerners come here lately to devote their lives to Amma and her service mission. They live at the ashram year-round, and many tour with her around the world. It seems to me this is what I should be doing. If I am to devote myself to my spiritual life, I shouldn't have to go back into the "world" every year. I don't like going back into the world all the time. I have no more attachments there; I have no friends or family that pull me back. Yet I feel a deep nagging inside. Honestly, I am not sure I want to be a full-time resident either, but I can't imagine doing anything else. Why don't I feel a simple desire to renounce my life and live at the ashram? I am trying to make sense of all of it. I have no home anywhere, so Amritapuri is my closest thing. I am confused, so I've decided to approach Amma with it. I write her a note explaining my situation (although I know she knows it all) and have it translated into Malayalam so she can read the note herself and not have to translate it while we sit here.

When Amma comes into the hall, I notice she is a bit irritable; she's not exactly shining with love and compassion. She has a scary look of the goddess Kali about her. Her skin is darker, and my little warning bells go off inside–uh-oh! Stay away! Fortunately, we get to sit for a while in meditation before I go up to her. But meditation is shaky for me, and I can't go deep. I feel a lot of trepidation and I wonder if I am doing the right thing.

But I have my note ready, so when it's time, I get up and wait for my turn in the line forming in front of her. I watch her as she receives the few people in front of me.

Suddenly, she glances me in the eye and silently warns, "Are you sure you want to come up here?"

Uh-oh, why am I doing this?

Yet something in me knows I must go through this, so I move closer. I must go; I can't stop this, even if I want to, and I don't know what I want.

I am in front of Amma, kneeling before her and handing her my note. She takes me into her lap and tucks my head under her arm, so I am lying across her lap with her arms resting on my back. I can feel her holding my note as she reads it. Suddenly, I hear her speaking in the microphone so everyone could listen to her. She is reading my note into the microphone! Every little secret, fear, and heart's desire that I poured into my letter with so much love and devotion, she is reading aloud to the whole ashram! OH MY GOD! In the note, I tell of my hardships in the West and how I just want to give myself to her and never leave her. I listen to her with increased horror. Her voice is dripping with mockery, like she is just saying blah, blah, blah, and she couldn't care less. There is a dead stillness as hundreds of people sit listening. I cannot believe this is happening. I want to die.

The blah, blah, blah of her voice ends, and she lifts her arms off my back, signaling for me to get up. She doesn't look at me when I raise my head to meet her eyes; instead, she looks away. Someone gently moves me over to the side of Amma's legs as the next person in line approaches the peetham. I have no sense of what to do or anything. It seems I am shocked out of my wits. I am sort of bent over next to Amma, and I stay there looking at the ground, crying tears of humiliation and a deep sense of something else–betrayal? That she didn't respond to me the way I wanted her to?

After moments of immovable numbness, I feel Amma gently push me to get up. I rise, and, with my head lowered in shame go back to my spot on the floor. I sit on my cushion and totally lose it. The silent wracking sobs are relentless, and I hide my face between my bent knees. I feel someone's hand on my back, which makes me lose it more. I can't believe she would do that to me. I can't believe she could be so heartless. I have watched so many come to her and offer her their lives, and she is so sweet and tender with them. I give her my whole life, and this is how she treats me? Why? I cannot think beyond the utter despair that I have lost hold of the one hope that I held onto–that Amma would call me to her and embrace me and give me a life with her.

Slowly, the loss of emotional control ebbs away, and I find myself able to look up. The girls are starting to get the food ready for distribution. The last few people are talking to Amma, and then the girls will pass Amma the plates of food. We will go up to her, and she will give us our lunch. I don't know if I can stand seeing her again; so deep is my hurt, my sense of betrayal. But I notice that the emotional edge is lifting, and the story is starting to fade. Something so intense is dissolving very rapidly, and I feel I am starting to get hungry. When the line gets a little shorter, I get in it and go up to Amma again.

I am standing in front of Amma. I am totally drained, but I also notice an absence of any expectation of her. I don't care at all. I don't feel any part of myself needing anything from her. Amma pushes my plate of food towards me, so I take it, and then she looks up at me with a sweet, concerned look and asks me, "OK?" The question goes right in, and I laugh.

Yes, Amma, OK.

Amazed at the effectiveness of whatever that was all about, I return to my spot with my blessed lunch. Only this time, I am laughing.

17.
Being Stopped

*Not only do I not know what's going on,
I wouldn't know what to do about it if I did.*

~GEORGE CARLIN

Have you ever thought you should feel more passionate about getting what you want in life? That you should have more drive to make something of yourself? Do you wonder why you no longer have any interest in what you used to love doing? This chapter may be for you. Being stopped is what happens when we begin to lose our personal will. Our personal will begins to dissolve out of our system as we surrender to the Totality, and a change of occupancy begins. This can be a touchy subject for some of you because we are raised in a society, within the 3-D world, where we use our will to create a fantastic life for ourselves.

Some of you may know what I am talking about, and this is because you are experiencing the dissolution of your personal will. You may have lost all passion for what you think you should enjoy. You may feel empty of the drive to create plans for a better future. The personal will dissolves as we evolve, and as the separate self dissolves, so does its will. It is the dissolution of the drive originating from "what I want my life to look like." We experience a dissolution of the drive that creates our identifications, which make us feel like somebody. We may experience an absence of any identification related to the world. When we lose interest in how we fit into the world, we lose the need to be someone. This may sound unsettling to you or even downright terrifying, but diminishing the personal will IS the spiritual journey.

The dissolution of personal will is a gradual process. In the old paradigm, as a separate self, we worked to keep the personal will strong. Of course, we were unaware of this, but this is what the ego drive is about—maintaining the identity or my will. The ego/separate self has a will that needs identification in the world. This drive gives us a feeling of security. A personal will enables us to have a plan, even if it is unhealthy.

Personal will creates the belief that you are the only one who can make your life happen. This drive keeps the self feeling separate, with strong individualism. There is nothing wrong with this; it is also a part of our evolution. But when the drive to find fulfillment in the world fails, and we experience dissatisfaction, we believe we have personal problems. We only see the relationship between the identity-self and the world. We don't look deeper. The illusion of a personal will disconnects us from the intimate relationship with the Divine Presence and separates us from a more profound flow of Life.

Everyone is experiencing a gradual diminishing of personal will, but most people don't realize it. If you have been aware of a gradual tendency not to have any drive to "make" something of your life, you may be experiencing a dissolution of personal will. Of course, there can be people with deep, unresolved trauma and unhealthy conditioning that can sabotage their personal will. Fear of failure can also sabotage personal will, which is entirely different. What I am speaking about is directly linked to the dissolution of the separate self. Throughout my life, I have experienced a noticeable lack of personal will–except in my spiritual life. I never had much interest in creating a career or a strong identity in the world, and at times, it was pretty unsettling because I also wanted security.

Many people can experience a lot of frustration around a diminishing will, as they feel they should have more drive to make something of themselves. We may know we have gifts to offer the world, but something different is happening. This frustration is very common, and if we don't know what it is, it can cause problems. It could create a new belief that we are not worthy or capable of success. We might turn on ourselves and judge ourselves, which puts more pressure on the nervous system. Unconscious insecurities can become more pronounced when we compare our lives with people around us.

Everyone is different here. I am talking to those experiencing a diminishing will, an emptying out of the drive to make something happen. I want to discuss this with you because you must understand what is happening. You are being stopped. Your "doer" is being disarmed.

Being stopped is another part of our evolutionary process that can cause confusion. But understanding this process and learning to align with stopping can feel like a great relief. If we have tried to find happiness in the world and have instead met with dissatisfaction, letting go of false hopes will bring a much-needed reprieve and a realignment with our soul journey.

The spiritual life can feel quite isolating at times, as it is a different kind of life. We don't have the same interests as many others, and since the spiritual journey is an inner journey, we begin to find it more fulfilling than most external activities. We may find ourselves alone. When the personal will weakens, feelings of isolation may intensify.

The absence of personal will can make it difficult to relate to others who operate from a personal will. We can't find ourselves in their experience, which is the basic connecting point in most relationships. This is what creates a sense of aloneness. However, this aloneness can also expose more of the grasping of the separate self.

Sometimes, we may feel an intensity of separation or an increase in density before a complete stop occurs. A complete stop takes place when the personal will completely dissolves, and not before. This is a slow dissolution, and understanding what is happening is important. The personal will may take a long time to dissolve, and it can bring up quite a bit of unconscious material. Dissolution of will is another powerful way to purify the mind, as the uncovered unconscious material directly reveals itself in the mind. We cannot control this process but can only align and cooperate with it. Surrender and devotion are our friends here, while attempting to control is not. Yet, we can allow everything if we remain conscious of the process.

Sometimes, the personal aspect of self tries to puff itself up again and do something about its life. It never worked for me, but it did try. The separate self wanted to feel some semblance of worldly security and "normalcy." It was frustrating because the separate self wanted a life, but there was no drive to do it. But it would try and fail. It was extremely challenging when everything the separate self tried to do failed before it even began. This period lasted for about 15 years and was a very important period of my evolution. The remaining shreds of my personal will only created ideas and thoughts; there was never any action behind them. I could feel something inside wanted something to happen, but it couldn't happen. This increased the dissolution of the separate self.

The personal will operates within the mind-body complex, so when our mind begins to recognize the patterns of its dissolution, there is a tremendous opportunity for the entire system to open. The pathways within the nervous system clear as we recognize the old drives as illusory. It can be a potent time to see that the old drives tugging at us to conform are created from an illusory self. We might find it funny that we have been trying to operate from such a futile illusion. We are now stopped–for the moment. Our system can now operate without personal will–through sensing and feeling. This is a place of incredible Grace: What we thought we were, an individual separate self, isn't running the show, so any effort is not coming from "me." It's coming from beyond us- from the Totality. There is much more space in the system, which can receive a different source of guidance.

Stopping is a great place to find ourselves; it is here that we can relax as our true selves. When the personal will exhausts itself, we have no choice but to let go. Not everyone is ready to be stopped, and we can't make it happen before it's time. The personal drives disappear in their own time as the system opens and consciousness awakens. A great intelligence is at work here.

When I returned from my last year in India, I sensed that my life was changing. During that last year (2003), I intuited deeply that it would be my last year, and yet I didn't know why this was so. I felt a completion of a process, even though there was no indication that I was "done" or anything like that. During that last year, Amma would give me these deep, extended looks, seemingly validating what I felt intuitively: that the most significant part of my life was about to change. I returned to the States in the spring and saw Amma in New Mexico that summer. My body was utterly exhausted from the intense drive of being a spiritual seeker. I had traveled to India for nine years, and it felt like I had been on a high-speed train ride that never stopped–like a ping-pong ball batted here and there. I didn't sleep or eat much then, as I was doing intense sadhana (spiritual practice).

That which had initiated the drive, in response to a deeper impulse, was the personal self, which was utterly exhausted. It was hitting a wall. The drive to be a seeker was being stopped, but I couldn't recognize it then. I only saw that my previous path of going to India to be with Amma was ending, and I didn't know what else to do. I didn't know how else to live my life, as being a seeker was all I knew. Seeing all this was quite disturbing because I still wanted God, but the way I searched to know God was finished.

I am standing at the back of the tent in Santa Fe, and Amma has just finished giving morning Darshan. A few of us are waiting for her to walk by on her way out. Amma walks right up to me. She puts her hand on my heart and says, "So tired." Just like that. My whole being responds to these words and the feeling of her hand on my heart, and I feel emptied out and spent. It feels like my entire being is collapsing inside. I walk over to a space on the floor and sit down. There is nothing else I can do. Something has left.

My whole body let go. I remember this feeling of total relinquishing, and the drive of the old way of seeking fell out of the system. Of course, I did not know this at the time. The personal aspect of self had lost the only identification it had left, that of being a seeker. It collapsed. The personal element of self had invested itself in its identification as a seeker; without it, it simply didn't exist. That identification was now nothing more than a fairy tale. Pure consciousness was no longer a seeker. The personal aspect of the separate self was gone.

I then experienced quite a bit of disorientation. There was an absence within my consciousness that wasn't there before. As a seeker, I had a purpose: to become enlightened. The separate self needs meaning; it needs a purpose to know itself. Even those who rebel against society's norm to go to college and get a career can turn it around and find meaning in their beliefs that they don't need that stuff. All beliefs can give us a subtle purpose if only we maintain the belief. At the core of the separate self is a tremendous insecurity and sense of lack, so it will look for anything to hold onto to hide the insecurity. So, without the seeker's job, the separate self became disoriented and somewhat distraught. Insecurity showed up. But the relief that my body and nervous system felt from being stopped was what I needed; I just didn't recognize it at the time.

Slowly, I began to enjoy the simplicity of life without the intensity of a seeker, and my being began to relax a bit. In that relaxation, I could sense a quieter flow that led me to my next phase of life.

About six months after the collapse, I was still attempting to figure my life out; things took quite a while to settle. And I remember feeling confused by the stopping: I kept trying to conjure images about my future to fill the space left behind by the collapse. My mind was concerned about making a secure and stable life, and it didn't know how to operate in a stopped place. Of course, at this time, I had no context in which to place the stopping; I had no clue that anything was different on the inside. I remember noticing that I wasn't as self-absorbed as I used to be. I had not had any previous exposure to the Western style of Satsang then. Without any intellectual understanding of what was happening, the mind couldn't relate to its experience. There was a disconnect.

Stopping can occur in several areas of our life. It can happen in our work, relationships, and favorite pastimes. Wherever there is identification, there is a personal will to maintain that identification, and when it is time, that drive will begin to dissolve. Some of these drives will fall off gradually and almost unnoticeably. We will realize that a particular way of being is no longer there. Other drives can be tricky, and these are the drives in which we have invested more. When these stronger drives dissolve, they can feel like a collapse of our existence–like dying. It is very helpful to understand what is happening. A guide or someone who has been through this can be extremely supportive. It was a full year before I could understand what had been stopped. The only obvious thing I could do was get a job and attempt to live a "normal" life. However, I was still deeply connected with Amma, so "normal" wouldn't happen.

My meditation became more of a time of deep nurturing for my spirit rather than part of the drive to get somewhere or have an experience. It wasn't until I sat with Adyashanti a year later that I began to see what had been and was no longer. It was an interesting first meeting with this teacher. I went and did a retreat with him in California, and on the first night, I sat right in front. Adya looked at me and said matter-of-factly, "Complete falling away of the personal, that is what has happened here." It was as if he was speaking about the weather. My mind understood instantly, and I didn't experience anything other than an understanding of the "event." I never once thought of myself as "awakened." It wasn't possible because it wasn't the truth. There is no "one" that awakens, ever. I tell my story for clarification so you can understand the evolution of consciousness. It is consciousness that evolves out of the personal self. And when this is genuine, there is no one to claim it. But this is not Self-Realization. I want to be clear: the separate self is still there, with all its impurities covering the mind.

When I began offering Satsang meetings, the separate self would subtly think it had found some purpose and "hope" for security through this new life. But nothing ever worked out for it, as the teaching work had plenty of new challenges. Fortunately, I never identified as a teacher; it couldn't have happened. The personal aspect needs to be there for any identification to occur. When I sat in Satsang, there was simply a flow of consciousness holding the meeting. However, there was a lot of energy during the talks. Afterward, I was just as human as anybody else.

The desire for security still showed up in my life, but without any drive to make it happen. This was the difficult part of this period. And even though I could recognize it, I could do nothing about it except surrender repeatedly. My devotion strengthened and matured during this period, as all I could do was open more to the Divine. My mind wanted some hope, but my Heart wanted the Divine. The teaching work kept exposing any "hope" for security, but the irony was that there was never any security in the teaching work. And because there was no security in teaching, the separate self kept trying to quit. I didn't like it much. Pretty interesting. As a result, the separate self had nothing to hold onto, which also kept the dissolution strong. For that, I am grateful. It would be easy for the separate self to hide as a teacher- if it provided security and a favorable identity.

Life, as Divine intelligence, can catch up to us when we are stopped. It's like the gallop of a horse that stops, and the dust cloud arrives a few moments later, surrounding the horse. The flow of Divine intelligence is meant to guide the mind-body complex, but if any personal drives dictate our actions, this intelligence takes a step back to allow the drives to run out. Divine intelligence doesn't try to impose itself on personal will. If the individual will is still strong, our intuitive connection to Divine intelligence will be faint and hidden.

As the personal will diminishes, it may be helpful to seek some support. We are mature enough to know what is truly important for us so that we can align with its process. We will look to strengthen our innermost connection with the Supreme consciousness. When things aren't working out how we would like, we become skilled at allowing our experience to open the system further. If we find ourselves stopped and confused, we can allow any confusion with compassion. There is no need to fight anything in this realm.

The more open we are, the more available we are for a deep communion with Divine intelligence as the flow of Life. This is the essence of our evolution, to know our most profound connection with Life as the Beloved. Life is just waiting for us to come back to it, back into its fold. Life is waiting for us to come back into the lap of the Mother, where all things are taken care of. Life only desires to care for its creation; we are not meant to struggle. So, until we are stopped, we cannot know this in the purest sense. We must be stopped completely to recognize how Life is taking care of itself. Then, our natural connection with Life will deepen.

Life is here for us to access its mysteries, yet if we believe we are in control of Life, those mysteries will be buried so deep that we won't even know they exist. When we connect to Life intimately, it reveals its magic to us. Life becomes fresh and new, and like small children, we become wondrously aware of each moment. We are completely open, without any idea about what may come next. We sense we are supported as we are guided into the rich depths of the Great Mystery, as this Mystery lives through us.

When stopped, we no longer need external recognition or validation; we discover the most precious in ourselves through our intimate connection with the Totality. There will be challenging days, as the separate self still looks for something to hold onto, but we will repeatedly find ourselves back in alignment with the Totality. Nothing is more precious to us, and slowly as we deepen, this Totality shows us this is the only way for us. Our journey transforms into deep faith, knowing that where Life goes, we are going, and we must see where it wants to lead us. We have lost our interest in a personal will and have no idea when or how that happened. We are happy to be rid of it because, in its absence, we realize what an obstruction it was. Our body and mind are much more spacious without any personal will, and we can feel the flow of life within as aliveness. A new Presence is exploring its freedom within our physiology. This might take some time, but the eternal is patient. We align ourselves with the natural order of the evolution of consciousness as we feel it is happening within us, as a complete change of reality.

18.
Failure vs. Fear of Failure

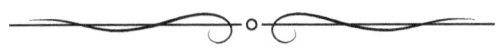

It is when you have tried and failed that you can truly surrender. Though you fail time and again, you continue to try until, finally, there comes a point when you accept your failure. You fully experience and understand your incapacity to move forward. It is at that point that you surrender. So, keep trying. That ultimate sense of failure must come to everyone, either today or tomorrow.

~Sri Mata Amritanandamayi Devi

The path of a seeker is a drive to get somewhere, to find something. The seeking drive is a drive that is looking for something special to happen because the seeker is an aspect of the separate self, so it is looking for some kind of fulfillment. And spiritual fulfillment can be an enticing promise of accomplishment. But we must remember that this seeking drive is also derived from Divine power, and it stops when its time is up. Stopping this drive and dissolving the personal will, which takes time, allows us to turn around and recognize the failure of the separate self. It is a good day when we encounter failure.

When we see that we have failed, we are reaching the end of a life; it is the end of a particular way of living our life, as it is the end of looking for something for the separate self.

Repeated effort has an essential place in the path of failure. There are a lot of folks in nonduality circles who love the concept of "nothing to do." That concept is valid from the enlightened perspective. When we realize that we are the source of everything, there is nothing to do to "get" it; what is true is right here as our Self. Yet, if we don't experience this as our most profound reality, understanding this concept and doing nothing isn't going to give us the desired result. It won't do us much good, as it's just another clever ploy of the separate self to stay in control.

Ultimately, we need an absence of control. We need complete openness. However, in modern spirituality, many spiritual concepts can be misunderstood. Misunderstanding without realizing it can often lead to false control. It can cause us to get stuck. This is why many concepts are dangerous when not under the direction of a competent guide. We need to be radically honest with ourselves at every step. We must see if we hold onto anything, especially our beliefs about our spiritual life. We must be so honest with ourselves that it starts dismantling those beliefs. We must be present and aware that this moment becomes the teacher, not the concepts in our head.

Using a concept or belief to design a convenient spiritual path is not the way to attract Grace. And we need Grace. While facilitating Satsang in the West, I heard many folks declare their understanding of a concept without having much self-awareness and understanding of themselves. They would repeat what they had heard and then follow that concept's rigid definition as a path without questioning its relevance to their own experience. They would fit themselves into the concept, like a square peg into a circle, which is not the way to liberate consciousness.

Questioning our beliefs can expose our attachment to spiritual concepts, and we can recognize how the separate self is trying to stay in control. This clarity is priceless. Questioning what we think we know is a powerful way to open the door for Grace, that vital ingredient towards ultimate freedom.

Constant effort is a way to attract Grace. Our efforts tell the Universe, "I am doing what I can to know the truth or to realize God, and I will continue to try until I breathe my last breath." Our continuous effort tells the universe we want to realize the truth of existence more than we want anything else. We want to be free. This is a very powerful message to put out there. The Universe listens and hears everything, so we must be diligent in our messaging. If we want a nice, easy "do nothing' process, the Universe has all the time to wait for us to get a little more on board. But if we are earnest in our endeavor to know the Truth, that intention begins aligning with the potential for Self-Realization in the Quantum Field. That message becomes a beacon of frequency, which, when done repeatedly, sets our priorities, and we begin to feel it in every cell of our being.

Our nervous system will start preparing to receive the Infinite. The hours of meditation and sincere prayer will shift our focus to turn more inward, greatly enhancing our ability to see the subtle illusions within our being. This turning inward from Awareness activates our inner essence to come alive. From habitually looking outwards towards what is eternal within us, this turn initiates the paradigm shift. What the Sufis call "Zikr" is the great turning towards the Beloved within. Initially, this turning happens through effort. Over time, the turning becomes natural and spontaneous as Awareness sees what needs to be seen.

Our evolutionary process happens within the mind-body complex. Many traditions recognize the value of human birth, but we quickly realize how short a lifespan we have. Amma says there is so much Light available, but our bodies cannot handle it, and all that Light would blow our circuits. Our efforts help prepare our bodies. The vast intelligence that initiates the spiritual impulse begins opening the system from within. This impulse is a grace, inspiring us to try to know the Divine. So naturally, we want our inspiration to remain pure. We do not want to pollute it with any intellectual concepts the separate self attaches to. Feeling inspired to try to know the Divine can be an incredible experience. When we truly love to sit in meditation, and our hearts begin to open, we can feel Divine Love begin to bloom within. All this beautiful inspiration comes from the Divine; why would we want to kill it with some intellectual concept? The Field responds to what is alive and genuine, and it is up to us to nurture it.

The vitality of our inner inspiration, the spiritual impulse, is the vehicle for our journey. The energy behind our efforts nourishes this vitality, which enhances even more efforts. It becomes sustaining even as the separate self creates hopes and dreams within the effort.

Initially, the separate self will think that it is making the effort. It will think that it is searching for the Truth and that its efforts will take it there. The separate self may also resist making an effort at times. It may become discouraged. It may leave one teaching or teacher and go to another. If the separate self moves around a lot, she probably won't make much progress. She may be looking for something other than the Truth, perhaps the fulfillment of a certain belief or concept.

But if the effort is constant and sincere, and the impulse within is nourished by continual effort, the seeker becomes strong and one-pointed. This is the energy we want—strong, condensed energy towards the goal. We want the energy to become so strong that it becomes laser-focused. This is the energy of a true seeker. This energy has a great magnetic field that absorbs the personal aspect of the separate self.

The personal aspect of the separate self is the seeker. It's her identity. We want to strengthen this, and the more effort behind it, the better. We want that spiritual identity to become so strong that it becomes rooted in nothing else. And that identity as a seeker propels itself toward the goal of self-fulfillment. The effort becomes the seeker's investment in an outcome. She pours her sweat and blood into the effort, and it becomes her world.

And then, one day, it is finished. The seeker identity cannot sustain itself anymore. This can happen in any number of ways, but the death of it is what matters. The Divine pulls the rug out from beneath the seeker, and she is done. It's a Divine set-up. There is no fulfillment for her. Without that promise, the seeker cannot sustain itself. There is no more imagined outcome. This is the failure of the personal aspect of the separate self. The tremendous effort it takes for the personal aspect of the separate self to fail is also a means for the evolutionary process to succeed.

Failure can take many forms; it doesn't need to show up in our lives as a spiritual effort. We can fail in our relationships, jobs, and self-images. Failure is like being stopped, but being stopped is the result of failure. It is the result of the identity hitting a wall.

Most people put more effort into their personal lives than their spiritual work. Most people invest years into their education and careers, and nothing is wrong with that. This is simply where the life of the separate self is at. The separate self that makes any effort to create a secure life is the same as the separate self desiring to get enlightened. It's still Divine power that is behind the effort and the result. However, the personal aspect of the separate self is believing in its own efforts and not those of the Divine power. We want to change that experience, so we know it is the Divine power that moves us.

Divine power inspires the effort, but the separate self imagines the outcome of the effort. This is important to recognize. We want to become sensitive enough to feel the Divine power moving us. Inspiration comes from the Divine power within us. The definition of 'Inspiration' comes from the root word "in spirit." Inspiration is the impulse behind effort, initiating constant action.

The personal aspect of the separate self may cause a deviation from the original Divine impulse. This deviation is the desire to get something from the effort for the separate self. Desire can pollute the effort for a while and may even stop the original impulse. If the separate self wants to be special, someone spiritually enlightened, and it doesn't happen, the original Divine impulse can die. But the false spiritual identity can remain- without any inspiration. The separate self has sabotaged the original Divine impulse because she didn't get what she wanted. This is unfortunate, but it is also part of the failure. Any desire for anything is a false drive to control so that the separate self feels secure. It's a deviation that can't harness the energy we need behind the seeker.

If we don't follow the Divine impulse to its end, we can end up anywhere; there is no guarantee for anybody. But if we genuinely want to know the truth, we will experience the strong impulse from within, as it nudges us and prompts us towards the goal. If we have a competent guide, that guide will continue to inspire us to keep going. This is so valuable. Pure devotion is a solid foundation that ensures that we remain inspired. And pure Love for the Divine greatly harnesses the energy for the seeker, propelling her deeper into her efforts.

The seeker's effort sends the intention into the Field, and the Field responds by creating just the right circumstances for the seeker to fail—because it is failure that the seeker needs. This is how the dissolution of the personal aspect of the separate self occurs. This is how a huge chunk of ignorance is removed from the system. Now, all that focused, condensed energy is freed up within the system. This is a powerful moment in our evolution, which initiates the transformation of the internal system.

After years of intense efforts, the seeker failed when Amma placed her hand on my heart. The personal aspect had reached its demise. The guru's Grace ended its life as a seeker. There was now no threat of any personal agendas getting in the way. Any continued evolution could not be "owned" by the separate self. She couldn't see anything special in any experience or awakening as it didn't belong to anyone. This great collapse opens the door to reveal that it all belongs to the Divine.

As you can imagine, this is a crucial point in our evolution. We will continue to go deeper into the mystery, and if no one owns it, the Mystery will reveal its hidden treasures. We are open and available to continue evolution within our system. This evolution will continue to dissolve the separate self. No one owns any of it, even though the separate self experiences it. Ownership is absent due to the collapse.

We will all eventually encounter failure on the spiritual journey. It may be in this lifetime or another. But it may not look like anything you can imagine. My first big failure was so obvious once I could see it, and it all made perfect sense. Once a failure has occurred, we can look back and recognize what didn't work. We can see how the separate self had hoped for a result and didn't get it. We can then let go of the separate self and its hopes for something to happen for itself. The energy that is released from the failure will free up consciousness.

The separate self thinks that if she just gets this one thing, it will make her happy and make her feel more secure. Since the separate self is driven by feelings of incompleteness, efforts to feel better will be behind most of its actions. There is nothing wrong with this because it eventually leads to ultimate failure. And it is this failure that makes us look within for something more lasting.

Failure can happen at any time and is part of life. Not everyone is ready to recognize failure, so they won't encounter the absolute stopping of the personal will that accompanies total failure. Recognizing failure allows us to be conscious of the stopping of will and can give us tremendous clarity about what has failed.

The experience of failure can be a challenging place to find ourselves because it can dissolve so much in an instant. A collapse can feel quite disorienting for a while. It's disorienting because prior to the collapse, we were operating on a plan. We will do this and that and get this result. The separate self loves these "plans" for fulfillment, but we may be left in the dark when the plan fails. The invitation is to allow this feeling of disorientation to deepen in the nervous system. The disorientation tells us that we are shifting paradigms. Without a plan, there is nothing. Allowing the complete collapse to be felt all the way tells the brain that disorientation is safe. This can be super helpful. Sometimes, this feeling can feel intense, as so much energy that made up the personal aspect gets released. All the energy behind the effort, the plan, and the desired outcome is suddenly released. I've noticed my mind stopped working for a while after massive failures. It's not pleasant or easy to be with, but if there is a total collapse, then you're ready for it. It's not one of those nice, blissful experiences. It's raw and brutal, and it feels just like a death. Let it happen.

The hope for enlightenment can contain some holy and noble ideals for the separate self. This is common. One of the things to notice is that there is "specialness" when it's attached to the separate self. But if there is a total failure, then all that specialness can be dissolved. If the spiritual impulse inspires us, we must follow its path until it ends, and then we can encounter failure. But you won't see it coming- that's the power behind complete failure. It's the failure of the separate self. It's the dissolution of ignorance. And now, what's left? More space, less self.

Failure is the door to complete surrender. Each failure allows us to sense the invitation to let go. When Amma put her hand on my heart and said, "So tired," I encountered a kind of death inside; the intense drive behind effort had reached its end. I didn't understand it as failure at the time, but I did feel it. It was like the whole self collapsed in on itself. I collapsed with it. There was nowhere to go and nothing to do. The drive vanished. It wasn't until a couple of years later that I learned what had happened, and it made perfect sense to my mind. Then I could get on board with it and allow what needed next to reveal itself instead of trying to make something happen. This was the paradigm shift. We cannot be ready for the second paradigm until the first one finds completion. We must experience utter failure so that the system can adapt to a new life of surrender and openness. One that is empty of special knowing. Failure brings with it a long-awaited rest after years of hard toil.

We have arrived at a moment where there is "nothing to do." This concept can now apply (although you probably couldn't care less about it now). But we're not done yet! Because the separate self is still with us, with all its fears and insecurities. But the identity is beginning to relax a bit more so that we can gain more clarity around it. Divine inspiration will come again at the right time, and we will be moved again toward finding fulfillment. We're already in line for the next set-up to fail. But after the big failure, this will feel a little different, and if the seeker has fallen away, the movement may be for something different. We may try to create something for the separate self, something more secure. And so, we will embark on a new venture, only to eventually encounter more failure and the continuation of the dissolution of the separate self.

It may sound like a drag- this dissolution stuff. And at times, it can be painful, for sure. But as we learn to ride the waves of failure, we better understand what is happening and align with it. We know what's left behind is far more valuable than what the separate self hoped for. As we lose all the grasping and clinging that is the nature of the separate self, our minds become pure and more able to reflect the immeasurable awesomeness of the Totality.

We might not encounter complete failure in this lifetime, but we must follow each path as the Divine impulse inspires us. As we sense the inspiration to make an effort, follow the guidance, and know that our intention to know the Truth is sincere, failure and the dissolution of the separate self will happen. If we intend to be a vessel for the Divine, we will learn to listen in a new way to this guidance. The Divine knows how to dissolve the separate self most efficiently.

We may experience complete failure at the end of life, on our deathbed, but we will have made the effort, which is the fulfillment itself. If we do not make the effort, we cannot know fulfillment. If, on our deathbed, we can realize the futility of the self's efforts and recognize where the drive "to get" came from, that moment before death can be the best moment of our lives. We can let go of the separate self and be free. Complete failure is our spiritual friend, as it liberates consciousness within our being. It is the release of illusory bondage.

One of the biggest sabotages on the spiritual path is the fear of failure. It is an unconscious fear that we aren't going to make it. We may convince ourselves that the tests of life are just too tricky, and why try to know the Divine when we probably won't make it? A fear of failure sabotages any Divine inspiration to make an effort; it cancels it out. Fear of failure can lurk in the shadows of the unconscious, keeping our lives nice and safe without any risk-taking. But if we stay nice and safe, we don't change, and the Divine inspiration will dry up. We could feel ourselves stagnating with our internal life staying the same, which will eventually end the spiritual impulse for this lifetime.

We might hide from anything challenging and not want to leave our comfort zone. Fear of failure is one of the greatest hindrances on the journey of evolution; it is the separate self's resistance to the Unknown. We are not following our inner inspiration to go beyond the need for certainty. We stay stuck to stay safe.

However, fear of failure is also quite natural and to be expected; it may be a constant companion for many of us. Yet even though we may experience fear of failure, the Divine impulse can still inspire us to make an effort. We recognize fear of failure as an insecurity of the separate self, which is understandable in an insecure world. Fear of failure doesn't keep us from following inspiration because inspiration feels alive, whereas insecurity does not. We want to be free. Fear of failure is of the conditioned mind, and if we have a strong need to feel safe, then fear of failure can be significant.

Fear of failure can sabotage the journey, which keeps us from experiencing complete surrender. The separate self's clinging to the known is too strong and will fight against surrender. The sense of "I am doing" is the reality it is attached to, and it will take tremendous devotion to change that attachment. Without attachment to the Divine Totality, the separate self cannot go beyond its need to feel safe. It will attempt to stay in control at all costs. Of course, the Totality can come along and take care of things in its own way, which can sometimes be pretty difficult. Situations such as unexpected death, illness, and great loss fall into this category. But if our devotion is strong and focused, we can let go in smaller, less catastrophic ways.

The more we encounter failure, the more the tendency not to want to continue may arise. Maybe this is why so many people tend to stop at some point in the many "phases "of realization. Maybe people stop because failure is such a given that the separate self puts the brakes on. Or it may find another spiritual concept to hide behind. There may be discouraging thoughts, seeing it all as pointless. I've seen many people stop at different journey phases and find something else to do. The common element with these people is that they didn't have devotion, so no Love was calling them forward. And it's not that they didn't love the Truth in themselves, but it never evolved into Divine Love. We need Divine Love to take us beyond the separate self's attachments to the known.

At some point, the notions of success and failure disappear, and we no longer operate from any idea of attainment. There are no longer any ideas about what success might mean; we are simply aligned with how life moves. Success and failure only exist in the world of the separate self. They are from a personal gain (or loss) perspective and have nothing to do with a flow that is evolving and becoming conscious of itself. To succeed genuinely, we must see through and go beyond any ideas of success or any fears of failure. The separate self cannot survive when we go beyond the dualistic definition of evolution. The subtle tendencies of the separate self dissolve along with any promise of personal attainment.

Fear of failure is unconscious, and I have seen myself withdraw because of that fear. At the time, I didn't recognize what was dictating the withdrawal, but if I had been frank with myself, I could have recognized that I was afraid of failing. This fear of failure can become extremely subtle, but the stronger our Awareness, the deeper we will see it.

Fear of failure can give us time to adjust to failure and help us move through it. It can also give us a break from failing, as failure can feel quite discouraging sometimes—even though the discouragement results from not getting what we want. The most important thing is to stay devoted and connected with the Divine Totality, even when we're afraid.

When we open to the Totality, Divine inspiration can reach us. Even if there is fear of failure, the Divine intelligence knows precisely how to handle it. The important thing is to stay conscious. Know what's going on in the mind-body complex. Allow all the feelings to come. Staying present and allowing our nervous system to connect with Presence will keep inspiring us to remain open. By nurturing our devotion, we keep our intention strong and connected to the Field. Fear of failure might still be sensed in the system, but our communion with the Beloved becomes the most precious, and we will risk failure so that we may know this communion at the deepest levels. This communion is our inspiration, for it is made of Divine Love.

As Amma says, "Pure Love removes all fears." Fall deeply in love and allow your system to open to true devotion. The fear of failure will not be a problem but may be another reason to keep going. Use fear as a springboard; allow it to give you the momentum to let go as profoundly as this moment asks. Letting go to Love is letting go to Grace, which activates the Divine blueprint within.

Don't allow yourself to enter the entrapment of fear- it comes from the conditioned mind, which draws from past experiences. The mind cannot know where it is going, but it can awaken and recognize the preciousness of intimately knowing the Beloved Totality. Allow the mind to fall so deeply in Love that it loses all concerns with failure or success. Pure Love is the answer to continually keeping our evolutionary process on track and deepening. Falling in Love is the vehicle for true success, where Love's intelligence leads the way. This is pure devotion and takes us beyond all likes and dislikes. It allows us to be consistent in our process, even when we fail. Allowing our Awareness to focus on the eternal Self keeps our system open and receptive. Rest there and let the rest fall away.

19.
The Infinite Sea of Grace

Grace is openness.

By remaining open, you let go of your ego and narrow-minded views and allow Divine Grace to express itself through you.

~Sri Mata Amritanandamayi Devi

*M*arch 2006. I am at a week-long silent retreat in the Redwood Forests above Monterey Bay, California. It's a small and intimate setting with numerous meditation sessions and Satsang. I am so grateful to be here. The deep silence supports encountering my illusions and resting as Awareness. I have been back from India for about two years, and it is lovely to deepen my practice here in American culture.

It is morning meditation, and we are in the small hall, settling into silence. My meditation is starting to be powerful, and I am ready to allow myself to drop in as deeply as possible. However, after just a few moments, I hear a woman behind me making jingling noises. She is wearing those metal bangles from India that make little jingling sounds every time she moves, and she is shifting around a lot. She doesn't seem to be able to sit still, and the jingles create quite a lot of noise. I can't help but wonder if *anyone else hears this. The meditation sessions and the entire retreat are supposed to be silent, so I can't just turn around and ask her to be quiet. And because my meditation is starting to be so strong, I don't want to come out and disturb my practice. The jingling continues for the next 40 minutes as the woman shifts all around with an evident restlessness, and I find myself in a disturbed silence as my nerves react to every little jingle. My nerves are jingled.*

The next session after breakfast is the morning Satsang; I have entirely forgotten about the earlier meditation and look forward to the talk. I sit in my chair in the hall with my eyes closed, waiting for Satsang to begin. I don't notice the woman taking her seat behind me, but I do notice as soon as the jingling noises begin again. She is very restless, and every little movement she makes is audible. Holy Moly—can't she keep still?

As the teacher enters the room, my focus shifts, and I feel myself anticipating Satsang. I feel myself open to the entire space and the energy of Presence. As the teaching begins, the words transport me into a place of great clarity, as if I can see every little illusion within me. I don't hear what he is speaking about, as the words seem to bypass my mind and go straight into a much deeper place. My being absorbs the transmission of the teachings directly.

Suddenly, the woman moves behind me, and there is a distinct jingle of her bangles. The sound is poignant and crystal clear. The jingle sound has a transmission, too! The sound goes right into my heart. Suddenly, it hits me deeply that this jingle and the woman are God! My mind is not thinking of this as a concept; I am experiencing this as a truth. My belief that the jingling shouldn't be happening had kept me from recognizing this truth. The impact of this realization is so intense that I am left completely stunned. Oh my God! I can see the illusion of the separate self with incredible clarity as I, as awareness, wake up out of it. The separate self that thought the jingling was wrong was the source of my discontent, not the jingling sounds. I, as Awareness, am not the discontented separate self. The jingling continues behind me, and I fall hopelessly in love with the woman and her bangles with each jingle. It's God, and all I can hear is the most beautiful sound in the Universe in those bangles. I feel myself start to laugh silently. It's a deep, freeing laugh that includes my whole body, and I bend over and bury my head in my arms. The teacher has been talking the entire time, but I am clueless about his words. I am silently laughing so hard now I can feel my whole body shaking and freeing itself from the illusion it just woke up from.

All at once, I notice that the hall is very still, as the teacher has stopped speaking. I hear him ask out of the stillness, "Are you enjoying yourself, my dear?"

I look up, and the teacher looks at me sweetly. He knows what is happening, and all I can do is beam back at him and shake my head in total amazement at the significance of what I had just realized. I bury my head again, simply because it's all I can do and continue to relish the deep-felt sense that I was just touched by a Grace that came in all on its own, a Grace that I could never have hoped for, that showed me something that I would never have believed was possible. Grace had woken itself up.

The word "Grace" elicits a feeling of mystery. For me, it is a magical word. Grace is an essential element in the spiritual process that can create the most significant transformations. Grace is the unseen potential that we need to be open to. When Grace does show up within our consciousness, it adds to the wonder of the great mystery unfolding within us.

When the shift in consciousness occurred during the retreat, there was the sense that Grace had just come out of nowhere. It was not something that "I" did. I was sitting there, complaining about the woman and her bangles! Yet, because I was so open to the energy of Satsang, something was able to get in. And in the openness AND the Awareness of the irritation caused by the jingling sounds, a sort of alchemical process could occur. It wasn't like I was trying to transcend the bangles or talk them out of my experience. The truth was they irritated me, and in that irritation, a particular belief was exposed: the belief that the woman should be still and take off her bangles. That belief was at the forefront of my consciousness when the teacher walked in. And as soon as I opened to the transmission of Presence, there was enough space within consciousness for my irritation and the belief. There was a soup of possibilities because I wasn't trying to move away from anything and instead was wide open for Grace.

What shifted everything was Grace. It was the final ingredient added to the soup. Some folks say that Grace is our true nature, but while I can choose to rest as my true nature, I cannot choose Grace. Grace seems to come in all on its own, out of the blue. It allows us to recognize this mysterious transformative component as the deciding factor in any situation, the final magical drop that decides the outcome when added to the mix. Without Grace, there can be no significant change.

When we become aware of Grace entering and shifting reality, it makes us more conscious of it as a crucial component. It can be so helpful to be mindful of Grace. There can be a tendency to come in after a significant shift and claim ownership, thinking that "I" was the one that woke up or that "I" did it. If we are not careful, we can block ever receiving Grace again. To stay conscious of Grace is to remain aware that this shift was not "my" doing; this complete change occurred only through Grace. Without Grace, it could not have happened. Grace keeps us humble. Staying conscious of Grace allows the doors to remain open for more magic and removes any tendencies for ownership.

The spiritual path is wrought with challenges, and there are many pitfalls. One of the biggest pitfalls is the belief that "I" am awakened or that "I" had an awakening. We can use these words to describe an experience we may have had, but if we think it is "my" awakening, we may come from ownership. When I shared the bangle lady story with you, I only shared it to illustrate a point. It was not something that "I" did. The separate self believed that the bangle lady and her noises were wrong and thought she should be quiet. This shift did not happen to "me" as a separate self; it occurred through Grace to wake up the field of consciousness within me. It changed how I experienced myself in my relationship with the bangle lady and made me very aware of the magical potency of Grace. It felt incredibly liberating since the illusions that the separate self were projecting were causing suffering. Those projected illusions created bangled-jingled nerves. When the shift occurred, my relationship with the bangle lady changed radically. It was an incredibly enjoyable experience.

Being prone to Grace is the ideal place to reside, and it is up to us to sense what that might feel like. To attract Grace doesn't necessarily depend on what we do or believe. To be prone to Grace is an attitude. It's our inner approach to the moment and our attitude towards the Divine. All our efforts to know the Divine create our attitude. If we don't have the right attitude, Grace will not come. Small changes may exist, but the big transformative shifts depend on our attitude.

In our daily lives, we can be closed or open. We may be operating on habitual beliefs and opinions, or we may be open to the Unknown. Knowing whether we are open can be tricky, so I devoted an entire chapter to openness. If the bangle lady is irritating me, and I am trying to be accepting of her, I am not truthfully being open. To be open, we need to be open to what is happening within us. That is the doorway–the starting point. To be truthful, we must be completely honest about where the struggle is. Is the bangle lady responsible for my struggle? Or is that struggle entirely my own? Am I struggling against my inner struggle? Or am I allowing?

The mind will always look outside itself for the source of its struggle. It might find a bangle lady, but the struggle is still within us. For us to be prone to Grace, we absolutely must be honest. We can experience Grace when clueless, but that's not the same as being Prone to Grace.

Grace might enter our consciousness to open us up so that we become more aware of its mystery. This is what happened during my first big shift by the river. It came out of the blue. But I was also aware that my old life was finished. I was open to the Unknown and had no idea what was next. It was in that open innocence, which was an attitude, that Grace found me.

To be Prone to Grace is to attract Grace continuously. We live in the realm of Grace. When we are open and humble, we attract Grace. When we allow the struggle and know that we cannot think our way out of struggle, we are in the realm of truth. In this moment, we open to the Divine. We are open to the Unknown. This combination of helplessness, openness, humility, and devotion are the ingredients for our attitude. When we have this attitude daily, it becomes hardwired as a way of being. It is this being that is Prone to Grace.

If we keep convincing ourselves that we know how to get out of a struggle, such as I need to accept (go ahead and try), or by dismissing it in any way, we are merely bypassing. The struggle will return, and we will either become an expert at denial or gradually be whittled down to a place where we can be honest. Remember, only the separate self will resist the struggle and bypass it. When we get to a place where we can be honest and realize that we cannot control the struggle, we stop the illusion from continuing. We realize our helplessness, and we open to the Divine. We now have the right attitude. Maintaining that attitude is the way- all the way. Then, we will become prone to Grace. Grace is the element that goes into the heart of the struggle and dismantles it, like magic.

Maybe we've had many extraordinary experiences, yet presently, Grace is eluding us, and we may feel stuck. We have to ask ourselves why this may be happening. Why are we not feeling Grace? We can also be the humblest person and continually be saturated with Grace. To find our way, we need to find the right attitude.

Grace allows us to see things that no one else has ever seen. Grace is new and fresh. Grace allows us to find authenticity in our process beyond what anyone else is saying. Grace leads us to discover the richness and value of our essential nature, which goes deep within and changes our physiology. This deep transformation has nothing to do with maintaining blissful states or highs. It changes our need for any state. If we want to go beyond ourselves and what we know, we need Grace.

It can be tricky when we think we know how to awaken or go beyond ourselves. But this is where we are going, and if we think we know *anything* about what we should be experiencing, we are still in the known. We do have our past experiences: what we have been through, what we have seen, and what has worked for us. And all that has given us some wisdom. But we cannot hold onto any of these "ways" from the past as consciousness evolves. We must stay in the Unknown. We are not prone to Grace if we believe we know how to awaken. The effort of staying open, with the right attitude- knowing that we don't know- is staying prone to Grace.

I can feel it when I shut the door to Grace; it feels closed and disconnected. It feels like the separate self is in the driver's seat. But even feeling the disconnect allows me to open again. We connect with Grace through our honesty. Only through our discoveries of these grace-prone experiences will we see what attracts Grace and shuts the door to Grace.

This process of humility takes time and patience, and we will make mistakes. Don't ever think that the further down the path you get, the more experienced you will become, and you will never make mistakes again! Mistakes are a powerful way to attract Grace, as they elicit sincere humility. We will continue to encounter places within ourselves that don't conform to anything we have ever experienced, so mistakes are inevitable. This keeps it all interesting, too.

Yes, the risks do become greater the deeper we go. The enticement of "I know" or "I am more advanced" is a constant danger. These beliefs satisfy the separate self and can be a massive hindrance if there isn't a real Master watching over. Even then, the enticement of an awakened or advanced separate self lurks in the subconscious. To a genuinely mature being, a statement such as "I am awake" is meaningless. And a statement like that just gets in the way of Grace. It is not in the realm of truth. If the separate self is incredibly insecure, a claim might make it feel better about itself, but that is not where awakening comes from. Awakening is an essential shift when consciousness evolves out of identifying as a separate self. What is awakening is Grace. When we are aligned with what is taking us beyond ourselves, we are aligned with Grace.

This moment is where the magic is; this is where Grace lives. Remaining aware of Grace's transformative power keeps us conscious and on track. We do not want to get in the way of magic, but there will be times when we do. Thankfully, as we become increasingly more sensitive, we'll know when we are shut down to Grace. It will probably feel yucky. But as we evolve, this is how we begin to embody Grace; it is how we become what we are.

Evolved beings are extremely humble because of their awareness of Grace. They bow down to everyone as they recognize Grace in everyone. These great souls remain honest with themselves; they cannot be any other way–they reside in the realm of Truth. These evolved souls are also fearless, for they have discovered the Grace of their journey and remain steadfast in Grace no matter what others say about them. They have found the key that attracts Grace, and the Infinite has opened its doors.

When Amma was very young, many people in the surrounding village were against her and the loving way She treated everyone. Amma was born into a lower-caste fishing family in a deeply conservative area of rural India. Even as a young girl, she expressed overflowing compassion for all the suffering she saw around her, and she would do whatever she could to help those in need. This was unacceptable because of the local traditions; she was a young girl who should stay hidden from society until she was wed. But Amma would have none of that; she would remain faithful to her heart as she saw everyone as her child and also of God. It was incredibly tough for young Amma to have so many of her people against her, especially since she could only do what she was doing. Yet she also knew that this was her path, as challenging as it became, and so she kept following it. The focus and integrity of her journey have made Amma one of the most authentic sages ever to walk this Earth, and the power of her love has attracted and uplifted millions. She has embodied the flood of Grace that flows through her, and this Grace is an exceptional kind of Grace; it is the Grace of the guru. The guru's Grace is the highest form of Grace as it knows everything about the disciple and is only focused on bringing about the purest qualities of realization in that disciple.

Those who know the guru's Grace know the incredible intimacy of its power. The guru's Grace always looks out for us, guiding us deeper into the Unknown, where the guru knows the way. It can feel like this Grace is always with us, and if we remain open and honest, this Grace can take us quite deep. But the standards are pretty high. Grace is not here to save us; that is not its function, and it never meddles. We must take complete responsibility for our process. Grace is a precious gift; the deeper we go, the more we realize it. It leaves us in awe and wonder at its uncanny precision and timing. When we see how we could never have brought about the deep changes without Grace, we keep turning towards it with complete devotional gratitude.

When we are prone to Grace, we can sense that a vast, infinite sea of Grace awaits us. I always get the sense that there is a lot more magic where Grace came from. To sense an endless flow of Grace is a great incentive to remain open. Our system is designed for this vastness to flow through it. Sense your connection to this vast infinite sea; know that Grace is right here, waiting for you to open to it. Bathe in the sea of Grace, allowing it to lead the way beyond anything you have ever imagined. The false, separate self will have no place to hold onto when we are open to Grace. It's a place of no holding. Grace has a nature to flow unhindered and will expose the separate self and any of its agendas within our evolutionary process.

We have the entire playground of life to be curious about, and within our being, we have an infinite range of possible outcomes to see and know what moves us, and what is waking up within us. Staying open to these possibilities is our doorway for Grace. It is Grace that teaches us the correct attitude to attract its magic. And when Grace comes, it will set itself free.

20.
Untethered

When I let go of what I am, I become what I might be.

~Lao Tzu

I am on the phone with a dear friend who has been a student of mine for several years. I thoroughly enjoy our time together as I sense conscious-ness evolving through each conversation, and there is a deep resonance in how we share our experiences. Our conversations have a remarkable tendency to describe perspectives succinctly, allowing the subtleties to shine through with great clarity as we see them together. My friend is a writer who is fantastic with words. She is telling me about a new situation in her life that she is finding challenging to approach. She is completely grappling for words; I listen as she describes what she is going through. All I hear is "ah, uh, and um…" coming out, and I chuckle at the futility of it all. After a brief silence, she laughingly says, "I feel untethered." I gently invite her to explore that space, leaving her astonished at what the untethering reveals. I hear in her voice the newness of the place she finds herself in, a shaky awe. She laughs at the futile attempt to know where she is and recognizes the invitation to relax deeper into the field of no reference.

The conditioned tendency to cling is the unconscious habit of needing to find ourselves in a relationship with our circumstances. With every description, every definition, and every projection of what we believe, we find ourselves in a fixed relationship with Life. Life unfolds in a natural, organic way, and as it does, it offers us the sometimes-challenging invitation to let go of any fixed reference. When we surrender, we are not surrendering the circumstance; we are surrendering our need to control it; we are surrendering the controller. We surrender our need to have a defined relationship with our world, a fixed reference. We will experience circumstances that force us to give up how we maintain control. We may try to maintain a particular image of ourselves, a specific persona, and then life comes along and dismantles that image. We may hold on to a specific way of relating to the world because it is the only way we know how to relate, but if life is ready to untether us, those ways won't work anymore.

Being untethered is a loss of familiarity. We lose all our ways of referencing where we are in life. Those familiar references may have been pleasant or painful, but they still gave us a familiar world in which to operate. When we lose those references and consequently lose our world of familiarity, we are left without a way to find ourselves. We can become quite disoriented when we can't recognize our familiar selves. We may get a little freaked out if our previous perceptions gave us a real sense of ourselves. When we cannot find ourselves in relation to the world, we begin to lose our world and the person who believed that her world was real. To not be able to find yourself anywhere is a Grace. When moments of untethering come around, get curious about it; see it for what it is.

Being untethered can give us a feel for what complete surrender is. A true surrender allows us to see how we try to control our world, even subtly. We all attempt to control ourselves in so many ways. How I maintain control will differ from how you do because we relate to our worlds differently. Our separate selves have different programming; we live from different core stories, even if they are similar ones. Our attempts to control our world come from lots of past programming; the same goes for everyone else.

When we, as consciousness, surrender the controller, we dissolve the hidden programs that make up the separate self. We are weakening the familiar behaviors arising from need, lack, insecurity, and fear. These are the programs that make up the core story, and the dissolution of those programs is also the dissolution of the core story. We are liberating and transmuting deep insufficiencies, the very fabric of the separate self. Surrender, through allowing, is how we begin to dismantle our outdated ways of relating to the world. It is helpful to be curious about this process and understand what is being let go of. If we can see the familiar patterns that keep us in bondage, we can become more precise in our journey toward liberation. Needing to find a sense of self familiarity is bondage. We must see how we fight to keep our world familiar and real, as this is the separate self trying to keep itself real.

Awareness will be naturally attracted to seeing the controller. As consciousness prepares to awaken from a false reality, it will relentlessly shine on the controller. Divine Grace will create situations in life that expose the controller, the separate self. It's incredible to see how efficient Divine intelligence can be in freeing itself from all illusory identifications. The more awareness is strengthened through seeing illusion, the more efficient it gets. So, the deeper we let go of our need to control, the deeper Awareness can go to expose the more subtle tendencies of control. Seeing control brings even more clarity and openness into the system. Even if we are open to seeing control a little, this allows the light of Awareness to shine within. We won't be able to see everything all at once. It's not possible. The system is being prepared, which takes time, patience, and love. We are human, after all, and letting go of control will take a little coaxing from beyond.

The habits of control may not seem obvious much of the time; in fact, they may seem quite natural. Our programs have been with us for a long time, so if we act the way we always do, without any curiosity, we are not bound to notice. We must start by being honest about how we relate to our world. We must be curious about any "rules" we tell ourselves about life or our spiritual process. There are no rules. To enter an authentic relationship with the Divine is a relationship without any rules; this is what dismantles the controller. This enables us to open to the Unknown. A genuine relationship with the Divine is a complete absence of control, and then the Divine can become untethered.

We are not the controller. We are the pure light of Awareness that sees the controller. As Awareness, we will see how the controller sabotages our light and keeps us bound. Control is an unconscious habit, a projection of our insecurities that blocks the radiance of a free life. And that feels awful. Control never works, and trying to make everything perfect takes a lot of energy. When we see how the controller blocks life's natural flow, we allow a crack to open within consciousness. Grace enters, and consciousness wakes up out of the controller. We can then begin to see all the rules we have been projecting onto life and open to a life without "our" rules. Feel what it feels like not to have rules about your process of evolution. It's a physical freeing up within the system. When there is no controller, Life can be free to reveal the magic within this moment. When Life is allowed to unfold according to the Divine Blueprint, there is much more new space for consciousness to know itself.

Losing our tendency to control is part of evolution. We are losing the habits, beliefs, and outdated opinions that make up the rules we live by. When the rules fall away, the nervous system opens into pure allowing. Our perception of reality starts to clear beyond our self-created rules. Consciousness is waking up from the controller; as it does, it is accessing a reality beyond the limitation of self-referencing. The controller believed in a particular reality of perceiving from a separate self and, thus, created it. When the controller is absent, that reality no longer exists because the perception no longer exists.

As we wake up, we have much more space to operate from, allowing subtler habits to be exposed. I have seen many people shift out of their identification with the controller and afterward begin seeing the controller everywhere. When we are unconscious within a particular framework of operating as a controller, it is much more difficult to see that framework. As we awaken from that framework, we can see it more objectively and without the tendency to be bothered by what we see.

One of the most efficient ways to see the controller is through our sensing body, our nervous system. The inner controller feels like a controller; it has energy. You can feel it when engaged; it feels tight and contracted in the body. Controlling energy causes an obvious contraction. We can feel in our bodies when there is a drive to maintain a reference for ourselves. The doors of our Heart may close to build protection around ourselves. There are countless ways that the controller can be felt in our bodies.

Control is a familiar feeling. As we recognize a familiar pattern of control by sensing it, we awaken as consciousness. This is good news. Feeling familiar patterns is a powerful way to begin to awaken out of them. Within our nervous system, consciousness is becoming aware of itself.

When we are identified as the separate self, we also identify with the feelings in the nervous system. The feelings and the programs become what we are. This is how we begin this journey, and it's completely natural. We need to start somewhere. Identifying with our experience has allowed us to become more conscious of ourselves and our habits. But as consciousness wakes up from these old habits, something significant begins. The identification starts to weaken. We are no longer the habits of the controller but the Awareness that is aware of them. We will feel these feelings of the separate self for a very long time, and the more objective we can allow them to be, the deeper into the roots of illusion Awareness can penetrate. There will always be things to feel, and the correct attitude makes the feelings pure, without any control or identity. This is how we keep evolving.

Being curious about the controller can open us up. Curiosity attracts the Grace that's needed to see with clarity. Curiosity opens the door so we can see how the separate self tries to remain in control of its world. However, curiosity is also a powerful way to become aware of what instills curiosity. Seeing the controller as the separate self from Awareness is profoundly transformative. But when we become aware of the Awareness that is going deeper into seeing, then our journey becomes life-changing. We know that the Infinite is going into our being and changing everything. Every aspect of the separate self is being infused with consciousness. As a result, we get out of the way even more. The illusions of the separate self begin disappearing with more regularity and significance. And what is left behind is free and untethered.

As we become more aware of everything happening within our system, we become more sensitive. The deeper we go and the more we see, the more the field of consciousness within us blooms. We become untethered as we relinquish control and cannot reference where we are. We are a conscious field of Awareness that supports the untethering. Even though it may feel disorienting, a support system is in place. We shift paradigms as we lose even the reference of feeling untethered. Instead, we are the Field that supports the entire system. Consciousness is maturing, and being untethered is another step beyond the separate self.

This can be much more challenging than it sounds. It sounds wonderful, being all expansive and free. But the truth is, we will continually encounter places of fear, insecurity, and doubt as consciousness exposes all aspects of the separate self. Going beyond control is terrifying to the separate self as certain circumstances show up. But we need this to become a pipe, so understanding the controlling aspect is essential. Going deep into areas of fear is a powerful way to get familiar with the Unknown. We must do this gradually so our system can adjust to it. It allows the nervous system to keep opening to a new level of unfamiliarity. So, if life is taking you way beyond your comfort zone, consider yourself lucky–your system is preparing to adjust to a new paradigm. The conscious Field within your system knows how to embody itself.

As we become more sensitive, we become more aware of our capacity to be untethered. We become more aligned with the flow of Life without the need to hold on anywhere. The flow of Life knows us better than we do, so it will probably keep making sure that any subtle holdings within our system are exposed. We may also experience resistance in areas where we want to find something solid to hold onto. The separate self may still think it has a life and make plans to control things. If we remain honest with ourselves, we will feel the flow of life taking us through these "last holdout" areas, and we can keep opening beyond them.

Trying to find ourselves anywhere in the world is control; it is another way to hold on. Of course, we live and function in a world.

We may have jobs, relationships, and specific duties that we perform. If we do not hold onto these reference points to reference ourselves (i.e., I am a teacher or a spiritual person), we can continue to open through our system. If we are free of any identification with these duties, then our nervous system can be open to receive the Infinite.

Maybe we believe we are helpful or are here to help wake people up. This is still identification and can get tricky. The separate self loves these hiding places; they are seen as the more desirable ways to relate to the world. However, we are still using life to find ourselves. There are endless ways for the separate self to try and keep itself in existence by relating to its world. Fortunately, it is also the way consciousness is used to wake up out of the separate self. As consciousness matures, even our capacity to define ourselves will dissolve. Consciousness simply can't describe itself because there is nothing to tell. Consciousness also doesn't perceive the "other," so it can't use anything in duality as a reference. Everything consciousness perceives is seen as an appearance, not something separate. Everything is seen as itself. So, if we see everything as the same as ourselves, we cannot use it as a reference. The vast field of consciousness doesn't have a place anywhere; it is naturally and completely without reference.

We are letting go of our separate personhood and going beyond ourselves. This heightens our sensitivity tremendously. We may be guided by life beyond any reference. It might feel as if we are passing through a gateway–an entry point where we can't take any control with us. Sometimes, it feels like passing through the eye of a needle. If we find ourselves in this realm, we have probably let go of needing a reference to a great degree. In this realm, it can feel like we are being pulled into the void, where we sense the invitation to let go. We are letting go of our world; we are letting go of every personal desire within that life. Some folks may not want this invitation but see if you can understand what I speak of. See if you can feel it in your system. We cannot take anything with us through the eye of the needle. Just like in death, we cannot take anything with us. We can only take our love and deep devotion to this process; this is all we need. Feeling pulled into the great void is a blessing; we can feel the invitation within our nervous system. We honor this great invitation and align ourselves with the wisdom of the maturing, evolving consciousness of who we are.

We are gradually adjusting to a different way of being where we do not need to find ourselves in a relationship with the world. And in doing so, we become the world. It is a place of deep knowing, living from the subtle movements of intuition within our system, and not needing to know any outcome. We have all felt this intuition before; we are now learning to live from clear inner guidance. We are aligning with the flow of life as we sense it pulsing within our being. We are listening to the wisdom of the Heart that arises out of the deep silence of untetheredness. Continually, we find ourselves at a crossroads of choice: to feel the pull into this vast, untethered, pure place or go back to grasping for something we can know. The silent pull into the gateless gate will tug at us, and when we are ready, we will realize that this gate is within our being—the gate for the Infinite to occupy.

We now find ourselves in a never-before-ness, as an untethered perspective that is pure silence. We feel the fresh aliveness of each moment and a new ability to see with clarity and precision. We align ourselves with that precision; we are in absolute service to that which guides us. We are the train, the light on the train, and the track through the dark. We are the dark, and we are the passengers and the luggage. We are the journey and the impulse to travel it. Yet, none of this describes what we are or where we are now.

21.
Death of a Star

*When you become nothing, at that very moment,
you will become the All.*

~Sri Mata Amritanandamayi Devi

The dissolution of the separate self is a lifelong process, and it happens so deep within us that we are not aware of it most of the time. Yet, if we know that this is a crucial component of our evolutionary process, we can be mindful of how to align with it. If we are under the guidance of a realized master, we will have a profound and intimate relationship with Her. In this way, we can allow Her to work so deeply inside us, due to this relationship rooted in Love. This is not an easy process, but the stronger our devotion, the easier we can let go to it. This process can often be confusing and painful as the separate self experiences the loss of its reality, which is itself.

This chapter isn't for everyone. Maybe some of you might find it a little frightening. But if you are one of those people who are experiencing what I am about to talk about, you might find this chapter to be a great support. I desire to offer this writing in the hope that it helps those who are going through this process or are open to it.

Everything within the Universe is cyclic, and we can see the repeated patterns of matter around us. Looking at nature, we can see the patterns of spirals, crystals, and all kinds of geometric shapes endlessly repeating themselves. All of us are part of nature, and we all share the same consciousness. We can see much of what we experience in all other aspects of our Universe, and the deeper we go within ourselves, the more we can begin to detect our inner connectedness. Everything reflects everything.

One of the patterns we can begin to recognize in our process is the trajectory of dissolution or dissolving of our will. The personal will, or separate self, has tried repeatedly to find fulfillment in the world and maybe even in spiritual pursuits. If our design is ready to evolve, that drive will begin to encounter a familiar pattern of failure, along with doubt and discouragement. Does this sound familiar? The separate self has set itself up in looping cycles of hope, failure, and doubt, and even though it encounters repeated failure, it remains convinced that its fulfillment exists in the world that it knows. As we become conscious of these patterns, we wake up from them, yet they must still play out.

At the center of our universe is the separate self and everything it wants, hopes for, clings to, fears, etc. We know our universe revolves around this center, and when an awakening occurs, we can begin to see that this center is illusory. But the impulses to keep our world happy and secure will still operate from a "center." Over time, the personal will loses power, and the drive to find happiness "outside" begins to fade. Still, we believe that our security will be found in the world. The paradox is that we don't have the drive to find it, so we set up a camp, hoping it will take care of itself. There can still be a subtle expectation that "everything will work out." You may even hear your thoughts trying to convince you of this. The mind still operates in the only "universe" it knows.... That of the separate self.

In our larger Universe, yet still within the 3-D reality, stars are constantly being created and dying. A star has a tremendous amount of energy within it, and when it dies, all that energy becomes an enormous gravitational field or a black hole. Dissolution of the separate self is similar in energy.

We may begin to sense the possibility of losing this center completely, of what it would be like to lose all our expectations from our world. The center begins to fade as it loses its capacity to believe in its world and itself. There is no energy to maintain itself as a center, and it can go through a dying process. As it collapses, the hazy center loses its ability to project outward in time, hoping for a future. For most of us, this process of collapse usually takes quite a long time, many years. During this process, Source consciousness matures and gets to know itself as the inner Being, which, for a Bhakta (lover), is the Beloved. This inner recognition can be incredibly exhilarating. Awareness continues to increase efficiency in seeing all the subtle ways the separate self tries to stay separate. It's an essential time for evolution.

Before a star dies, its mass becomes exceptionally dense. This is the star's gravitational field, which is beginning to change and get stronger. As the separate self within us begins to dissolve, we might feel an increase in density. It almost feels like we are feeling all our stuff more than ever. There is an increased awareness of everything that makes up the separate self. We might feel increased fear, doubt, and confusion as the center loses its capacity to believe in anything. It can feel almost desperate at times. We might be sensitive to a feeling that feels like a death or an ending, and this feeling might stay with us for quite a while. We must watch any thoughts that might interpret these feelings as despair or hopelessness. This is almost to be expected; the limited mind can only see an absence of hope as the center loses power.

As the center fades, our true inner Being strengthens, pushing all the beliefs supporting separation to a conscious level. Consciousness is blooming within our system, and we feel everything much more acutely. Any feelings of separation will now be experienced differently, maybe more painfully, more densely. If the separate self feels fear and doubt, it will be impossible to push it aside. These feelings are powerful entry points that consciousness uses to open the nervous system even more, and because they are dense, they are full of energy. These deep-rooted feelings of the center are some of the most potent ways that consciousness can access and embody this vessel. And it will continue to use them to do so.

The energy that is triggered by density can feel like agitation. We might experience an edgy, nervous feeling as the brain perceives the Unknown. Remember, the brain needs to feel safe, and the Unknown doesn't feel safe now. But this will change. We must allow all these feelings space without expecting them to go away. The mind might look for the cause of these feelings and even blame itself for not feeling more peaceful. The brain perceives all this dissolution as an unknowable danger and begins to be on high alert, sending messages of danger in the form of nervous or agitated feelings. See if you can show the brain what is happening, sense the star's density as it is dying, and allow the brain to understand the process as it is taking place. The brain loves to understand things, which will help reassure it (somewhat) that we are safe. This will allow the process to go all the way through. Be gentle with yourself, spending time in quiet and solitude. The center of our universe is dying, and not many people around us are going through this process, so giving ourselves whatever we sense is being asked for is very helpful.

When aligned with our process, we can sense within our being that which is dissolving and reaching an end. We can feel this star-self nearing the end of its life, as it has repeatedly encountered failure after failure, and in doing so, consciousness has stopped believing in it. The old identities are fading away. The old hopes and empty promises fall off like leaves off a tree. It feels organic and intelligent. The drive towards any future fulfillment is being completely dissolved. If we are tuned into this process and have been for many years, this sense of nearing the end of life can feel quite intriguing. We might desire a final dissolution, yet there may be apprehension simultaneously. The true inner Being and the remnants of the separate self share the same mind, and we will witness a dance back and forth for a while.

Of course, it is not life that ends; it is the imaginary center of life that ends. It is the end of all the ways the center projected itself onto Life and how it believed that Life should accommodate those projections. After living with it for so long and seeing how it is the cause of all the pain and suffering in the world, you would think it would be an easy thing to let go of. But we are letting go of the only way of being that we have ever known. We cannot understand what is on the other side of dying, and like any other death, we simply know that it is happening. And just like any death, it will be different for everyone.

As dissolution increases, our lives can sometimes become quite simple. Consciousness dissolves how we might want to hold onto old relationships, activities, and pleasures. We might lose interest in many things that we believed gave us fulfillment and joy. There may also be a "clearing," which is an energetic adjustment to a higher vibration in consciousness. In my life, I lost my day job, which had given me some structure and something to do every day. It was evident that life wanted to let it go. And because there was a complete absence of a drive to do anything else, life became quite disorienting for a few weeks. There was no movement to go out and look for another job, and I had yet to learn what was next. I found myself without anything to do (which the star life needs), with no money or plans. Shortly after, I went to see Amma, and she played with me with the chocolate kisses, completely unhooking my mind. For weeks after, the mind had nowhere to land, and as a result, there was a noticeable increase in density, causing extreme agitation at times. But I knew intuitively what was causing the density; I knew about the deaths of stars, and I could sense that this star was dying.

When real stars die, their gravitational fields strengthen, pulling everything around them into themselves. It is said that when our star dies in our solar system, it will pull the closest planets into itself, annihilating them.

As the separate self within our system starts to dissolve, we lose interest in our "old" world. We don't seem to believe in it anymore; paradoxically, we may feel the pain and suffering of the world even more. We may become increasingly more aware of the world as if we are pulling the rest of humanity, animals, and everything else into our awareness. When the center fades, there is only the Totality. We may feel much more connected to others, even though we may never say anything to them. As our center dissolves, we become more aware of our true nature, which includes everything.

This moment is sensed as the only place to be, and our connection with Totality becomes our most valued relationship. This most precious connection is the only thing that will transition through the final dissolution, so we allow our alliance to strengthen. For many years, I lost tremendous interest in much of anything; I was only interested in this connection with the Beloved Field. I still enjoy nature, as it is the one place where all the old habits of the separate self are unnecessary. When hiking or camping alone, I become deeply aware of the Infinite moving through and around me.

We will undergo a great change if the inner Design is allowed to unfold. It's essential that we don't apply any concepts to this unfolding.

Our lives will become emptier and emptier of things that we may be tempted to hold onto, and there may be periods where there is nothing to hold onto. People can also disappear from our lives, and since we have lost any drive to cling, we may find ourselves very alone. This can cause more agitation. Just know that agitation is another symptom of dying. It can feel like we are isolating ourselves when the divine presence draws us in. It can feel like we are trying to go in opposite directions simultaneously, as the Divine impulse lets go of the old ways, but the separate self wants to hang on- especially around relationships. This, too, can cause agitation, so we want to continue to show the mind what is happening. And we want to remain open and allowing. We show the mind that this moment is the only place to be. The star-self slowly fades as more space is brought into the system, dismantling any tendency to cling to the old ways.

When we find ourselves at the threshold of death, we can intuit that it is a rarified gift. We are in a place that is only accessible through deep surrender to the Unknown. We find ourselves on the edge, or what feels like an edge, and we sense that we have never been anywhere like this. See if you can find the place inside your being that intuits where you are. See if you can sense what is on the other side of this threshold, not in a known way, but in a way that feels like an invitation. Feel the profound, silent invitation to stay still and not move away from the threshold. Let what is irrelevant disappear, leaving more space to open to the Infinite. We might find ourselves at the threshold repeatedly, so it may begin to feel like many little deaths.

The threshold is a place where the mind can get disturbed. The first time I explored the absence of a future, my mind kept trying to come up with options; it kept running horizontally, looking for a way through. But at that time, the center self wasn't ready to be completely let go of; consciousness was just getting the mind used to the idea. Consciousness prepares the entire system so that it won't be such a mind-blowing event when the central self is ready to fall away. Evolution isn't meant to be cataclysmic within an organism; it is gradual and almost undetectable. It becomes ordinary (which is not what the central self wants). The mind becomes a little more comfortable with the threshold; it begins to understand what is taking place, although it can still want to know how things will turn out. The mind starts to see that figuring life out is not up to it, and things get very quiet. The mind loses its capacity to even think about what will happen. The depth of stillness begins to envelop us, and our nervous system soaks it in.

Working with the mind is helpful, as the brain needs to understand what is happening (as much as we are able). To illuminate the mind with understanding allows it to recognize that it is part of the evolutionary process. The mind can begin to see that the dissolution of the central self is an extraordinary event, and it, too, wants – with some trepidation – to see what is on the other side. Since the source of the mind is also consciousness, the mind is evolving into clarity. We find ourselves waiting as we sense it is just a matter of time. With this attitude of waiting, we feel that our old way of life is finished, that the foundation of our world is changing, and through that change, all the rules also change.

One of the ways the loss of the central self changes the rules is that we lose our old ways of perception, how we label and define everything and everyone. We define others through our perception of them, not as they are. So, everything we perceive is interpreted through this central self, whether ugly or beautiful. When this central self begins to dissolve, we begin to lose our capacity to analyze, which is a welcomed loss. Of course, we may also experience an increase in density around analyzing and interpreting as the loss is happening, which can be uncomfortable. It's just the mind getting cleared out. Stay conscious and allow it to happen.

When we lose the central self, we have a much more realistic perception of life. We are no longer looking from one point in the universe towards another. When we lose seeing from a fixed, conditioned perspective, we gain the entire field; we become increasingly more aware of the totality of existence and feel more intimately connected.

When a real star in the universe finally dies, it leaves an immense space of nothingness or a black hole. This antimatter space has an enormous gravitational field. If you have ever seen an artist's rendition of a black hole, you will see the central space closing in on itself, surrounded by a vast galaxy of matter. Where the star used to be, an enormous gravitational pull attracts the galaxy towards it. New rules are beginning to emerge in the absence of the star. If you look at a black hole, you get the sense that the emptiness of the center attracts everything to it. Just by being what it is, this emptiness of matter attracts all matter to it.

Some cosmologists theorize that black holes are like gigantic tunnels leading to other parts of the universe. They are like big pipes. When Amma calls herself a pipe, she implies she brings precisely what is needed through her Being. She attracts matter to her. In the early days of the Ashram, there was no money to spend on extras, and sometimes the residents had to skip meals. Amma gave Darshan in her parent's cow shed in the early days. There were a couple of huts for visitors and ashram residents. That was all there was to the Ashram. There was barely enough room for visitors, and Amma often slept outside so visitors could sleep in her hut.

There came a time when some donors came forward with enough money to build a new temple, which would add new facilities to accommodate the visitors and give Amma a proper place to receive her devotees.

This new temple was about to be built when Amma heard about an orphanage nearby that was in big trouble and would soon have to turn hundreds of orphaned children onto the streets. Amma didn't hesitate to use the temple money to buy the orphanage instead, thus saving the children from losing a home. She was operating in the moment and responding to what was relevant. When some residents heard of Amma's plan, they immediately thought the temple would not be built because of the lack of funds. When Amma heard of their concerns, she told the residents not to worry and that God would provide for them. The next day, two truckloads of bricks showed up at the new ashram site just before the workers began the construction. This happened out of nowhere, which is how the Quantum reality works- in the Unknown. There are countless examples around Amma like this one, each defying the old rules of how we think and understand reality. Amma is a massive pipe of great compassion, and her vast humanitarian projects have been completed this way. Amma attracts anything to her that is relevant at the moment. If she hears of a village in Africa that doesn't have clean drinking water, she will attract the resources and the technology to fix the situation. All She has to do is think of what She wants to see. She is a massive pipe for the Totality to work through.

When we live as the center of our universe, we are the "doers', meaning we think that we are the ones that make stuff happen. We are the ones that act. Through that action, we get an imagined result. When our "doer" dies, the rules change. As the center dissolves, we lose our drive to "get"—the personal will dissolves. We lose any drive to make anything happen; we aren't interested in it. But we still may feel agitated about not knowing how things will turn out. Our only option is to open and question, with inquiry: *What is agitated?* When this dissolution happens, we need to separate ourselves from that which is dying. We must repeatedly let go of that life as this will be the process.

As we let go of the old life, there might be a natural inclination to ask ourself the direct question, "Who am I?" This is when this question is going to hit home. Many people use this question at all stages of dissolution, but when we sense the density of the dying star, we will want to open the door for the true inner Being, the Supreme Self. Use this question for this means. Ask it. This is the most potent time of our evolution—don't sit cowering and shaking in the corner because your world is dying. Be courageous and step into the Unknown. Be what you are.

The death of a star changes the rules. We start to feel ourselves becoming a space that is opening into infinity. We are becoming without any limitation or containment. Without a personal will, we are now ripe for the Universal will to come through us. We can sense the reality shift if we sit quietly and allow ourselves to receive. We are here to be a vessel for the Universal Will to shine through, and we will know the difference between the two realities.

The more the separate self dissolves, the more we lose our tendency to doubt and worry because we lose our capacity to think about the future. Doubt is very common to experience while the separate self is fading away. But as we lose our capacity to think about the future, we become increasingly more aware of our deep connection to this moment through a felt sense. The presence within our being connects to itself in the flow of Life all around. It draws to it what it needs, as relevant. When we operate from the central self, we can't imagine attracting the way Amma does, even though we may sense that possibility. The mind's old way of operating is to know what it wants and then think about how it will get it. As we lose the separate self, we lose that way of thinking. We lose self-centered thinking. Our thoughts become more universal as they are sourced in Universal Will. We can sense the invitation to allow this new way in, which resonates deep within our hearts and nervous systems.

Our aspirations change along with the rules. We might have an idea that originates within our mind, but it will feel more like an inspiration or a spark. When this inspiration sparks within the mind from Universal Will, it is called a Sankalpa or a divine resolve. A Sankalpa has tremendous power. A Sankalpa is the awareness that this "idea" is already happening in another place or dimension. When pure and free of self, a true Sankalpa can bring forth what is already happening in another dimension. It is a way to broaden this reality into other possibilities, which is how creativity works. We bring forth when we create. But remember, this occurs due to an absence of a separate self and an alignment with Universal will. The separate self cannot create, as creation comes from the Totality.

Amma attracts thousands of people to her, so she does not think about what she wants; she thinks only of her children. She sees everyone as her children, and within each one, she sees pure potential. She makes a Sankalpa to bring that light out, no matter how many lifetimes it might take. She has made it so because of her Sankalpa because this truth already exists. Somewhere, we all know what we are.

As the central star dies, we lose our tendency to cling or push away. Our likes and dislikes fade away. We will not lose all this at once but gradually become more aware of it as the old paradigm shifts. The death of a star is the death of an old life, and we have no idea what the new life can bring. But we have Amma as an example, and if you know her life story and where she came from, it is a fantastic example of what is possible. Each of us is a star with the certainty of dying as its natural design so that a new life will emerge.

I invite you to sense this infinite spark of potential within you, the same spark that created the universe from nothing. It is a spark that is empty of any center, and because it is empty, it contains everything within it; from every little blade of grass to every fantastic possibility that can ever exist, it is all within that spark within you. The spark that inspires you to let go and die is the same spark that gave you your life. You began as a pinpoint of nothing before even light existed, and from that pinpoint of nothing, an entire universe was created. This spark inspires you to be curious about life, and you are becoming increasingly aware of its source. It is a spark full of hope—*not* for our life as a separate self—but for our evolution as consciousness, in which the separate self is absent. This spark will ignite as a Divine impulse, to evolve and explore its potential, without a center.

22.

Tantra and the Art of Receptivity

Whatever is received is received according to the nature of the recipient.

~THOMAS AQUINAS

The ancient philosophy of Tantra is the art of receptivity. It is the sacred union of the infinite spirit with the realm of physical form. The philosophy of Tantra has many different translations, yet at its purest and highest level, it is the descent of consciousness into the physical body. In the Christian tradition, it is known as the Immaculate Conception. When we consciously allow presence to enter our being, we are experiencing the true essence of Tantra. When we are receptive, we are open and allowing to that which, by its very nature, is waiting to occupy.

When I began spending a lot of time in the wilderness, I could feel the presence of the trees and the mountains as they shared their essence with me. Everything in creation gives off a subtle transmission. In nature, it was very easy to feel a Presence and to receive and connect with it. I would just open to Presence, and it would enter into me. It was so deeply satisfying to feel connected with all that beauty, and I intuited that it understood me. I felt a deep kinship with nature because it knew everything about me and what I was going through. Nature became my first true spiritual teacher, and I longed to spend much time alone with her.

When I first travelled to Amma's ashram in India, there were no English translations of Amma's talks. Amma would speak in her native language, Malayalam, a complicated language to learn. I figured that if Amma had wanted us Western devotees to hear her talks, she would have provided us with translators. Even in the old days, many Indians could speak English. So, if Amma wasn't concerned with us hearing her talks, it must be because we didn't need to. There was another way to receive her teachings. Being with Amma felt like being with Nature, and I knew how to open to what she was sharing.

When I first began to sit with Amma, it was very easy for me to be receptive to her presence and to tune into her energetic transmission. Amma's transmission is potent, and her children are meant to receive her teachings directly through transmission. Many years ago, she once said that it is not up to the teacher to awaken the student; it is up to the student to be receptive. Receptivity is a quality of absolute openness. It attracts Grace.

In the early days, I would watch other Westerners ask the English-speaking Indians for a translation after a talk. Of course, I understand the desire to know what Amma was saying! But whenever I heard a translation, it always felt disappointing to me. It felt inferior to the silent teaching that I had been basking in. I soon stopped trying to get any translations; the words seemed to diminish the deep connectivity that I felt in the silence.

These days, all Amma's talks are translated, and that's fine. In her talks, she often seems to give the mind nothing to feed on, as if she is waiting for the disappointment that can follow an intellectual application. Intellectual teachings can leave us empty energetically, as the only satisfaction comes from mentally understanding the words. But some people enjoy that kind of intellectual satisfaction. But for the rest of us, we are looking for something deeper. We need to discover another way to receive a teaching. The energetic transmission coming from a Great Mahatma is massive, and many people will notice it even before Amma enters the hall. Learning to receive that transmission is another way the nervous system evolves and releases old programs. Learning to allow the silent teaching to go straight to our inner essence is an important aspect of being a disciple of a great master like Amma.

Our systems are designed to receive. We are simply open and allowing the ever-present to connect with the true essence of our being. There is an absence of a person trying to figure it out or get a particular experience. When receptive, the separate self is absent so the transmission can find its target. Being receptive allows our nervous system to sense the true inner Being. When we are receptive, we can feel the Totality, which informs us of its infinite nature as a felt-sense. If we are closed and trying to get something from life or a teacher, we are entirely in the way of what is being given, and there can be no connection.

Receptivity takes great humility and courage. It gives us nothing to know and hold on to. But at the same time, it can also be immensely satisfying for the same reason. Receptivity is pure connection with Source. When we are receptive, there is no place for any personal agenda to make demands. We are not receptive if we are making any demands or have expectations. If we think we know anything, we are not receptive. Receptivity is a deep feeling of being entered by the Unknowable.

I have heard stories from people who met Amma say that they never felt anything from her; she just seemed like a lovely lady giving hugs. I have seen people become angry because there is so much activity and bustle around Amma. But these are many ways Amma exposed the separate self's limited understanding. I have heard people criticize the busy energy of selfless service that accompanies Amma on all her tours. These reports leave me dumbfounded, as my experiences have been entirely different. I do not know why these people had such completely different experiences as I have had, but I do wonder if these people were open and receptive when they were with Amma. It is so easy for the ego to project onto a teacher what they think the teacher should be like. If we grasp for or project onto any teacher, we are bound to be disappointed, and we won't be able to receive that teacher in a way that could be beneficial.

There are two types of receptivity: that of the world and that of the Divine. What I am speaking about is receptivity with the Divine. It is an energetic exchange. Divine Receptivity is when our system allows energy to enter, and in that, we attract. When we are open, we attract Divine Grace, like a lover would attract the Beloved or a flower would attract a bee. This attraction is very natural, and only our beliefs block this natural attraction from happening. When we feel receptive, we open the entirety of ourselves to the infinite vastness of this moment. We are not making any demands, and we are not looking for any kind of experience. Learning to become receptive removes obstacles so we can feel a deep intimacy with Presence. We naturally want to open even more when we feel this intimacy. And the more we pay attention to Presence, the more we evolve as a vessel to receive.

To receive the Infinite into our being can feel quite profound. At first, we can sense in our system that what we are experiencing is only a tiny fraction of what is available. As we evolve, the system's capacity to receive naturally grows, and it begins to realize its capacity to receive. The system naturally opens further, allowing the Infinite to come in. Our system is designed for this, so when it receives the Infinite, it is like a key fitting perfectly into a lock.

This magical design of the formless entering form unlocks the mysteries of existence; this is the essence of Tantra, Divine Receptivity. A decisive shift happens as consciousness descends into the depths of our being. It is *pure* conception. Just as when the sperm enters the egg, there is a miraculous genesis. Egg and sperm are no longer individual entities but have joined to create something entirely different. As consciousness descends into physical form, the vessel begins to live a new life with a new conscious function. This is the key to awakening consciousness, which ushers in a new way for our physiology to identify as. This shift in identity alters the nature of the vessel as it slowly loosens its grip on the separate self. Each time our being is open to receive, the key slides into the lock. There is the dissolution of the old as we receive what is new.

As the vessel evolves, it shifts paradigms. One of the most radical shifts lies in the way we think. The separate conditioning thinks linearly, such as if I do this and that, I should get a specific result. It is a linear, mental trajectory creating a horizontal, flat existence. The spiritual seeker also thinks that if she just does this and that, she will become enlightened. All her problems will be solved, and she will be happy. This paradigm has layers and beliefs supporting its linear mental projection. If everyone around us thinks in the same linear way, then we are probably not so inclined to try something different. But don't worry; if consciousness wants to awaken, it will shift the paradigm. All we need to remember is to stay completely open. The receiving takes care of the rest. We will watch as layers upon layers of dense illusions within are exposed by consciousness as it descends. These are often revealed as thought patterns the brain creates to keep us safe. Oftentimes, these thought patterns have a sticky tendency towards seeing fault or danger in our external environment. Consciousness will make these patterns visible, and we, as Awareness, can witness their fantastic transformation. This has been one of the most remarkable experiences of my journey: watching consciousness remove the dirt from my mind, as the brain begins to lose its old habit of perceiving danger. This is the power of Awareness, and it will become more efficient as it descends into the illusionary constructs. We receive the descent as a lover receives its beloved, with no demands whatsoever. As we receive, we are actualizing the purity of our devotion to Truth.

Of course, this is a process, so it doesn't happen overnight or even in a few years. It takes time and tremendous devotion. It's a lifelong commitment. It is the process of fitting the key into the lock and forging the opening of the lock so that the descent of Consciousness can enter through and through. This is the embodiment process, and even though some people prefer to believe that there is no process, we'll all be able to recognize that we're not free. Indeed, consciousness is already everywhere, but we will be able to recognize how awakened it is within our own being. We will be able to discern if it is free. If we still feel separate, our embodiment process hasn't reached a mature actualization. The descent of consciousness is a process of actualizing consciousness within the mind-body complex. If we feel separate, the descent of consciousness hasn't gone deep enough. But when we are open, we can feel our physiology receiving the Infinite consciousness. We can notice the changes within the mind. This experience and these changes can potentially leave us in awe and wonder, as the descent becomes more and more noticeable. This is a consummation of the highest order, and it leaves no room for the small, separate self.

It feels safe to receive the Infinite because the brain can perceive that we are not alone. The mind-body complex has a Friend that understands it completely. We have never had that before! As consciousness penetrates the body, we feel connected to the greater whole. The more receptive we become, the more we can feel how consciousness allows the body to feel at ease, even when other emotions arise. So, taking time to feel the receptivity within your being is conducive. This is our physical design; the more receptive we are to the Totality, the more aligned we will be. We gradually lose the self-interests of the separate self. We are not thinking in a linear trajectory; instead, we are open to the vertical descent of Consciousness, which will radically shift the paradigm of "me and what I want and don't want."

As consciousness wakes us from the dream of the separate self, our systems naturally let go of the old way of relating to circumstances. When we are in the grip of our agendas, holding onto people or things, we experience grasping and clinging, which tend to feel tight. This is because, at the time, the nervous system is tight. The nervous system channels are restricted, so there is not much room for the flow of Consciousness to recognize itself. When an awakening occurs, if it is authentic, our nervous system can begin to open, and the grasping becomes less frequent. The decrease in grasping allows the system to become more receptive. Receptivity is a natural function of our nervous system that develops as the separate self dissolves.

When our nervous system receives, it receives silence and depth. It becomes increasingly more sensitive to information inherent in silence. This is the source of intuition, psychic abilities, energy healing, and actual knowledge. It is the source of inspiration and wonder. To feel silence and depth informing our system is to feel connected with the source of life. We become sensitive to a great Love that is supporting our evolutionary process. We can sense that great intelligence guides our evolution, and gradually, we learn to trust it. We sense that this intimate connection is our most precious relationship in Life, and we become more attached to it, our true nature, our Divine Self.

As we experience the unfolding of Self-Realization, the recognition that our true Self is emerging in its self-recognition, we experience an indescribable awe. We know that we are in the middle of a shifting paradigm. We want to nurture this profound change within. The more receptive our system becomes, the more we want to receive. The process becomes a delightful dance of being informed by the Beloved of the purest Love. We want nothing from the Beloved except to receive the Beloved. As our system receives the Infinite, we feel a great intimacy with the entire creation—as if we are receiving Love.

This deep receptivity transmutes the vessel of old insecurities, and a profound personality transformation occurs. Often, we won't even know these changes are taking place; we simply recognize the absence of old patterns. It is such a relief to be free of these patterns that we naturally open even more to the receiving. What we are receiving is making room for itself by dissolving what is obsolete in our system. Our system begins to recognize that it is a physical manifestation in an infinite reality, not something separate.

As we bear witness to our evolutionary process, we sense that this process has the potential to go far beyond what we can imagine because we *can't* imagine it. Receptivity keeps us in the Unknown. We feel the silence being received within our system, yet it is not of the quality we have known before. This is a different paradigm. It cannot be spoken of (even though I am attempting here), and because it is the Unknown, putting any mental constructs about it is impossible. We will know what we need to know when the time comes. It is the infinite's natural design to receive itself. Just as Shakti receives Shiva, the form receives the formless. What is ultimately true in us receives itself.

We are an evolving species with an entanglement of every human tendency possible. We begin to have a new relationship with our human tendencies and can start seeing them as opportunities. We see them as open portals for the Infinite to enter and occupy. Our weaknesses, or vasanas, become a way, not an obstacle. If any part of our humanity is meant to change, it will be through being receptive. We all have our inherent design, which is precisely what the Infinite brings forth. What is being received is creating an utterly authentic vessel with its unique blueprint.

Your authentic vessel will be different than mine. Diversity abounds in nature, yet it is all pure expression of the Infinite. There is no such thing as a perfect tree. But there is a lot of "treeness," with crooked branches and twisted trunks. When we allow Consciousness to enter our being without any idea about how we should feel, we lose the division that dictates how we should feel. In its place, consciousness can pour compassion and tenderness into all parts of our being, allowing a great coming together–a whole and healed human.

As our system recognizes the innocence of its humanness, another quality naturally reveals itself. In the absence of any inner division, we become naturally attractive. Our beings become the means to attract what is relevant to this moment. Babies are a great example here. Babies are naturally appealing. When we see a tiny newborn, we want to connect with it and get close. The baby doesn't think of itself as attractive; it just is. A baby attracts simply because division is absent in its little being. A baby cries when hungry or tired because it is natural to do so. And when the baby cries, it doesn't wonder if anyone will come. It cries as an expression of a natural need, and the Infinite shows up as a loving parent with food. Its needs are being met as needed, and the baby cannot wonder if any of them will be met in the future.

Likewise, we attract what is relevant to the moment, and as our vessel matures, we will become incapable of imagining ourselves in the future. We are designed to receive what is appropriate right now, so there is no place for the "future." As we evolve, we lose our capacity to worry about the future. And if we do not think about the future, it ceases to exist. This moment reveals its potency–what is contained here and now. This moment is the doorway that a conscious, undivided Self can access.

Another excellent example of attractiveness is Amma. In the old days, we all tried to be respectful and follow the tradition of the guru by giving her lots of space. So, when Amma walked into her yard or the temple, we would all step back, even though we wanted to be close! Nowadays, everyone rushes towards her, not because they are disrespectful, but because they can't help it. Amma naturally attracts her children to her—like bees are attracted to the sweetest nectar. Many thousands of people are attracted to Amma's sweet fragrance of Divinity. Many of these people are attracted to Amma in a very intense way; it is inexplicable.

Sometimes, it takes a lot to crack our system open enough for it to recognize its capacity to receive. Hidden deep in the subconscious, there can be so much self-judgment and division within our being. It's been there for a long time. Deep down, the separate self doesn't like itself much, it resists its own human frailness. But as consciousness awakens, it begins to meet all the old programs from the past with deep compassion, transforming them. Consciousness might do whatever it takes to open us up. It might hurt; pain is a very effective way to crack open any protection the separate self has in place.

Somehow, we must begin to see how the separate self maintains its separation; only then can we be free. Consciousness is freeing our entire being from experiencing itself as separate and into a vessel that can receive the vast Love of the Infinite. Consciousness doesn't judge what it sees within the vessel; it can't. As the consciousness within our system wakes up, *we* begin to experience an absence of judgment because the self that judges is dissolving. The inner division is fading away. As the paradigm shifts, we align more and more with the evolutionary opening of our being. We know that what we are is what's opening us. One of the loveliest qualities the physical system begins to feel is a new tenderness and patience with itself. The brain understands why the inner division has been there and gets on board to experience profound healing into Oneness.

23.
In the World, but Not of It

The purpose of our life is to realize our true nature—infinite happiness. Do not miss out on the precious opportunity to find your eternal, blissful Self by running after temporary joys.

~Sri Mata Amritanandamayi Devi

June 2000. I sit beside Amma while she gives Darshan in Santa Fe during one of her summer programs. I can only see Amma for one day to save money to return to India, so this day is precious to me, and I don't want to miss a second. This is my sixth summer returning from India, and I have been working like crazy. Amma looks at me, smiles, and says in Malayalam, "How is everything in your life?"

In the early days of my sadhana, in the late '80s to early '90s, when I was going through a lot of emotional purification, I had a very peculiar notion. I experienced a lot of emotional pain in those days and didn't have the skills or maturity to know myself. Often, when we don't have the skills, we want to escape, either through relationships, drugs, materialism, or God. And so, I thought I could leave this Earth if I could know God or become Self-Realized. I didn't want to live on Earth any longer, even though there were parts of it I loved. I didn't relate to its rules and felt very separate from everyone else. I used to pray to God in my moments of anguish when I felt so alone that "I want off." I used to pray relentlessly, how I wanted to "come home." It was a very intense feeling. I wanted off this ride on Earth. My idea of merging with God didn't include this world; it took place elsewhere.

When Amma asked me that question in Santa Fe, my mind turned on itself. I considered the phrase "my life." I felt like Amma was telling me something; it felt more like she was giving me something. She opened my consciousness to a new possibility... "my life." And that was the beginning of breaking free of any ideology that dictated that I needed to give up something to know God. She also pointed out that my life was fine despite its specific challenges. I was sitting here with Amma and making money to return to India to be with her. I wasn't having as many difficulties as I had encountered in the past, and my basic needs seemed taken care of. Things were looking up.

This began dissolving the belief that I needed to be with Amma as much as possible. I didn't realize it then, but she started giving me "my wings." The seventh year in India, 2001, was the first year I spent in Ramana Maharshi's ashram in Tiruvannamalai, where I stayed for two years (with a summer break). During that time, my mind would get confused about why I was drawn to Ramana's when Amma was in India. Yet I was moved to be in the energy in Ramana's Ashram, and that time was potent for me. I would spend hours every day in the meditation hall, and my sadhana began to be influenced by Ramana's teaching, which started me questioning everything I thought I knew.

Eventually, Amma called me back to her in Amritapuri, but something had shifted. I had my "own" journey, a new way to discover God or my true Self. Of course, my heart still wanted to be with Amma as much as possible, but I knew intuitively that my relationship with her was changing. She was giving me a direct link with my true Self, which was an absence of my old self–that self with limited ideas about the way to Self-Realization.

When I returned to the West after my final year in India in 2003, that long-felt desire to escape life was absent. The personal aspect of the separate self was no longer present, which had influenced the desire to "come home" (which to me meant somewhere else). I did not see it dissolving; I just noticed its absence one day. I was glad to be rid of its burden, as that tendency for escapism had been with me my entire life. I knew my time in India was over, so there was a readjustment period. I got a job working in a Natural Medical office, and shortly after, I got a loan and got a decent car. Finding a more permanent place to live took about six months, which was challenging. It was my first winter in Colorado in nine years, and it snowed like crazy, so I froze all the time. I was settling into something new and completely different. Some of you may think that this is something everyone does in the world, so why is it worth noting?

Life is about flow. Some of you may have experienced times when your life suddenly changed direction without you knowing how the change happened. Maybe one minute, you are in love with someone and want to spend the rest of your life with that person, and then suddenly, you are entirely done with the relationship. Or maybe you feel passionate about your career, and then one day, you completely lose interest in that work and can barely get out of bed and go to your job. Well, the flow of your life has changed its course. It can be disorienting if you have a radical flow change, like doing something you had no previous inclination to do.

So, going from following a path that excluded the rest of the world to following an impulse to settle into the world was odd. That first year was quite disorienting. It felt like part of me was still going in one direction, and the new part was going down a road that I had never known was possible for me to go down. Yet, I sensed that this was the next step in my evolution. I knew on a deep level that I was ready for something else. My entire adrenal system was fried, and my body was cooked from all the intense tapas. The thought of returning to India was gone because my seeker was gone. Being a seeker was the only identification I had known, and because it was no longer there, I was living in the world without the drive of a personal self. I had no drive to "get" anything.

My life became simple. At the time, I didn't have any concepts of awakenings, loss of personal self, or anything like that. I had yet to attend any Western Satsang, so there was no concept to apply to "my life." I felt a settling taking place, and there wasn't any drive to do anything different. However, I did notice that I didn't "seem" like other people, and I was curious about that. Other people seemed motivated to do and get things, and I could see that they thought doing them would make them happy. I also noticed that many people would say things about themselves to define themselves and unconsciously look to others for validation. I could feel a lot of insecurity in some folks, mainly in the people I worked with. When I found myself unable to relate to others because of how they related to themselves, it left me even more disoriented. All I wanted to do was settle down and relate to the rest of the world, but there was still a gap.

After I sat with Adyashanti for the first time, much of this confusion started dissipating. He helped me understand what was absent in myself, which calmed things down. I was coming from a different perspective than the rest of the people around me. I had lost the capacity to think I had found or accomplished anything. In spiritual groups, I noticed that some people would talk about their awakenings or experiences, but I couldn't do that. It was absent. But I still tried to relate to folks by going "outwards," trying to connect to them. It didn't work so well, not in a way I could feel. I felt odd in the world, like a fish out of water. It wasn't until consciousness began to mature and know itself deeper that I discovered that the way to connect with anything or anyone is by connecting with yourself, the true Self.

I was in the world now, but I was not of it. I couldn't look for validation from others as to who I was. I tried to do this, but it never worked. I didn't feel a drive to accomplish anything to substantiate myself. My personal drive was absent, yet I found its absence a bit troublesome: my mind interpreted this absence as a lack of motivation and laziness, and my body responded to this interpretation by feeling lazy. In those first years back from India, I had no concept of the dissolution of personal will either, and so the absence of drive made me feel like I was floating without any direction. I only wanted to be simple and settled, so I continued my daily meditation, went to work, and came home. I still had the old drive to work as much as possible (like I was still going to India), so I had two jobs in my first two years and waited tables a couple of nights a week.

After I had met Adyashanti, I would listen to his recordings often and see Amma when she came to the States. I also sat with a few other Satsang teachers and could feel an affinity with them through their heartfelt presence. When I was asked to teach, I initially resisted the idea. I only felt the desire for silence and simplicity. I didn't feel any urge to sit with groups of people or share any teachings, mainly because I didn't feel I had anything to share. After being asked to teach several times, I decided to talk to Amma about it. So, when Amma came to New Mexico in June of 2005, I got in the question line to ask this crucial question.

When I got up to Amma's side, she was attentive and incredibly loving towards me. She kept rubbing my face and smiling at me for long moments. When the Swami asked Amma my question about teaching, she suddenly became very serious. At first, she told me some interesting things about Western teachers, which I still remember (but won't share). Then she told me to be careful who I sit with to avoid diluting the (Amma) transmission. And then she told me a little story, which caused the Swami to laugh quite a bit. I can't remember the story because my mind had completely shut down by then, and I was stunned (Amma can cause this sometimes). But I remember how it made me feel. The story translated into how everyone hears and understands teachings without investigating themselves. Amma was very serious, and she kept looking deeply at me. Then she told me, "Wear your own pants, don't copy." She wanted me to find and explore the truth without ingesting others' interpretations. She wanted me to stand in my own autonomy and authenticity.

At first, I was startled by Amma's answer to my question. Honestly, I imagined she would give me heaps of support and make it evident that she wanted me to start teaching. But that wasn't the case at all. Her answer confused me. I remember feeling disappointed that she didn't give me a clear and concise answer. Yet, later that day, as I was sitting in front of her on the floor, Amma passed on her Dharmic transmission (an energetic transference that I will not describe). It was an authorization to teach, but I still didn't equate it with having her blessing. Because of the confusion, I didn't start holding Satsang until about six months later. My confusion- thinking that her blessing needed to look a certain way–blocked me from recognizing her bless-ing. Then, one day, I heard Amma's voice saying, "Amma didn't say no!" At this point, I had forgotten any idea about teaching and didn't care if I did. The Infinite led me to ask Amma and showed me that I did have a slight attachment to teaching, wanting her to give me her blessing, and then I was given the time to dissolve the attachment.

I needed to be free of any expectations around teaching to remain detached and aware of my needs to keep growing.

Amma's instructions for me regarding teaching were somewhat cryptic to my mind. The mind wanted solid answers with clear instructions, something it could feel secure with. It wanted an "Amma endorsement." Instead, Amma put me on a somewhat challenging journey of discovery, the discovery of how to "find my own pants." The path of a teacher isn't all it appears to be. I could go into this in great depth, perhaps in another book. But it is not just sitting in a chair and giving Satsang. It is its own journey, and if one can stay open, one can use this path as a teacher wisely. This has been my process since 2006; twenty years later, I am beginning to discover my own pants. (Side note: I stopped offering Satsang in 2020 to give my full attention to my journey.)

Our lives are incredibly precious; we all have within us our unique design to be discovered. Yet many people copy everyone else, thinking that is the way to personal fulfillment. It takes openness and sensitivity to find your own way. To be "in the world and not of it" is not easily understood; it must be discovered. You only know it when you are in it. It's like you are marching to the beat of a different drum; the guidance of your wisdom is born out of your inner silence. When we embrace the depth of our stillness, inner wisdom begins to reveal itself.

We become stopped in time by letting go of our need to know the future. We stop while the rest of the world spins around us. In this stopping, we become deeply sensitive to our inner guidance; we begin to "know" how to live, even when the mind doubts. We are discovering our own pants. Deep within, there is an intelligence that does not come from the typical drive for security or even the drive for some spiritual experience. This inner intelligence will not reveal itself until all redundancy is removed. We cannot copy others' words or actions. At a certain point, we leave all concepts behind and enter vast availability. We are being moved from an absence of any drive at all. What is moving through us is a flow beyond any remaining notion of separation. It is a flow that knows precisely what it is capable of and moves towards its fulfillment within its design.

When we experience life as a simple flow, we only engage with what is relevant to this moment. We are not moving from a drive to get something. When we engage only with what is relevant, we can then experience completeness in this moment. We don't feel any lack in ourselves when we recognize this moment as complete. Yet, as consciousness matures, some sense of incompleteness will remain, which we may interpret as our lives not quite right or a relationship that's not quite right. If there is a sense of incompleteness within ourselves, we will project that incompleteness outward. This is only natural. Consciousness is finding hidden places within that still feel separate. We will continue going through this as consciousness wakes up and the separate self disappears. The flow of life will expose many insecurities and weaknesses; this is how our inner design is accessed. If we remain conscious of what is happening and devoted to its vital process, the flow of life within us can move through all obstacles of weakness and fear.

We can only find wholeness through our connection with ourselves. As we recognize this and attach to our true essence, the light within becomes more luminous. To keep returning to our true Self, or innermost Self, is to strengthen a bond that will take us far. It is an eternal connection that nothing can ever take away.

Our world is beautiful; it is not something we should dismiss as only a dream. It is in this world that consciousness is waking up. When we connect with what is essentially true in ourselves, we also recognize what is true in the world. When we wake up enough to see that the world can never define us, meaning we don't find ourselves through our relationship with the world, we are in the world but not of it. When we are no longer of the world, the world appears as conscious, too. The world reveals itself as our Self.

There is a famous scripture: *"The world is Illusion; Brahmin alone is real; the world is Brahmin."*

First, we must recognize how and when we attempt to define ourselves through our relationship with the world. We may love our friends, but are we using them to define ourselves? We might be doing great service in the world, but are we using this to define our ideas about ourselves? These are the kinds of deep, honest questions to ask. Most folks live in a relationship with the world's illusory nature, meaning they try to find themselves through how they fit into the world, even if it is a spiritual world (which can be tricky). Some folks can rebel against the world and its social norms, yet they still define themselves by it. Only when we do not define ourselves by how we fit into the world can the world be free to be what it is. We can still find ourselves standing up for justice and what's right. But it has nothing to do with us. When we see that the world does not define us in any way, we begin to be free of its illusory nature. When we sense that the world is not what it appears to be, we want to be free of the world's definition of us. We want to know what is true. When we as consciousness fully wake up to our true nature, we know ourselves as Brahmin, and simultaneously, we know the world is Brahmin, too. We see we are the same as everyone else, even if they do not know it.

When we lose all our definitions of ourselves, the natural flow of life begins to be freed up. We no longer need to maintain any relationship with the world, so we do not place any demands on life. The personal will can block authentic flow, as the separate self's drives to get can feel like flow. But that is not a free, authentic flow.

Our life circumstances often oppose what the separate self wants, especially in the early stages of our journey. Any sense of lack within our system needs to be exposed before our life is experienced as a pure flow. Pure flow originates from the vast intelligence of Life; it does not come from our mind or ego's desire. It's a deep, instinctive feeling. Pure flow causes the flowers to bloom and gives the birds their song. Pure flow is how we are meant to live, in harmony with all of existence.

When the separate self sees that the flow of life isn't going to give it what it wants, pure flow can almost feel like dread. The flow is going in a direction that the separate self doesn't like. This is how you can see if the flow is pure. Even after consciousness has awakened, there will still be desires, so we must stay attentive to our conditioned patterns. Oftentimes, if there is still desire in the system, it is good to work it out, yet remaining mindful that it doesn't consume us. We must see that all desires, even when fulfilled, are empty. They cannot define us. A genuine desire is to find fulfillment, yet the separate self will still have its ideas about what fulfillment is. We are the vast sky of consciousness; the deeper this is realized; the emptier desire will appear. Soon, the flow will take us to our deepest desire, only to know the purest truth and be an instrument for that truth.

Pure flow feels clean; it feels empty of any expectation. When we are in flow, we sense it to be something being done, not something we are doing. We feel guided, and even as we are in the process of movement, we cannot foresee any outcome. We might intuit that a change is coming, but the mind cannot imagine that change. We can only be in flow in this moment, where we connect with our deepest essence. We engage with what is relevant to this moment. The mind's function begins to shift as its reflective qualities become clearer. The mind's new role is a tool in the hand of flow. The mind might be used to figure out the best way to publish a book or design a book cover, but the flow uses the mind to think about these things, rather than the separate self. If the flow is not moving toward getting something done, the flow will not be using the mind. If the Totality wants to give instruction, it may come through the mind as inspirational thought. But slowly, the mind loses all its drive towards empty desire and becomes a function of the Divine.

Flow becomes very simple because it isn't trying to create a future. Our lives become more spacious. It isn't because we have more time on our hands; it is because we are here; we are present. There is an infinite amount of space here. Our sensitivity is heightened as we deepen our connectivity with our true essence. We feel our life rather than think about it. We sense flow, and the more we sense it, the more efficient flow becomes, growing more instinctual rather than intuitive. We simply know what to do—we are not guessing and wondering how to decide. If we do not know, we wait until we do. Pay attention to that small knowing within. The more you pay attention to the small, intuitive sense, the more it becomes instinctual, and the stronger it will get. Trust your gut feelings, and give the thinking mind a break. You will often find the thinking mind in opposition as flow develops and becomes known to you.

As our lives become informed by flow, things naturally simplify, and we are much more aware of the beauty within the flow. Each moment shines forth as a blazing opportunity to be informed by the source of creation. Our bodies feel deeply loved and appreciated as the flow of all life moves through them. As we feel more supported and cared for within our physiology, there is relaxation and a new conscious alignment with flow. The system has harmony, balance, and a gradual ebbing of conditioned thought. The mind becomes less interested in anything other than what makes it conscious. The mind begins to recognize the source of its life. There can be a new feeling of enthusiasm and wonder as the body-mind senses what is possible when all separation is dissolved. Our physiology recognizes that it is a vessel through which the Infinite reality can be lived. It forgets its old ideas about being a separate person. Those behaviors have dissolved, even though we can remember having them. We have reached a "tipping point," where we cannot maintain the illusion of a personal separate life; we have lost the capacity to believe in that world.

Flow moves of its own accord as it knows how to use the vessel most efficiently. Flow is pure creativity that is always fresh and new. It is pure energy, and from this energy, all things in this universe are created and destroyed. Flow is life; we can either slow it down or free it completely, depending on how we allow it. Only our conditioned ideas about the world slow down flow. The absence of those ideas allows the flow to be free. Our systems are designed to feel the internal impulses—the wisdom within guiding us as vessels of flow. The more open to flow we become, the deeper we recognize that we *are* flow. Flow is evolution; it is the natural order of all Life. It is designed for efficiency and change, and what is inefficient dies off. Flow changes our human species, bringing us back into balance and connectivity with the Totality. We may encounter chaos within the flow, but flow knows how to bring out the best. It only wants the best in us. Because that is what it is.

24.
Alone with the Totality

The important thing is not to stop questioning.
Curiosity has its own reason for existing.

~ALBERT EINSTEIN

As long as I can remember, there has been a deep awareness that there is so much more to life than just what I perceived around me. I always sensed that there's much more information available to us than what we are accessing. I have often felt frustrated at how I related to "my life" because I felt capable of so much more. This was, and still is, the impetus behind my spiritual life. Yet, at the same time, amid frustration, I have known that my life is so rich with possibility because of this inner inspiration, which has kept me focused and on track. This inner inspiration has allowed me to let go of everything I thought I knew. Slowly, the frustration has been replaced with incredible awe and wonder as the Totality reveals its mystery.

As a result, my life is a tremendous opportunity to go way beyond anything I previously thought possible. I perceive separation as only programmed thoughts created mainly by psychological components, which I know can be radically transformed. The deeper I go into this mystery called "Joi," the more I see that an undeniable miracle is happening within. The deeper I go, the more capable I become of seeing the most subtle aspects of the separate self, mere holdings of psychological memories within the unconscious realms. Hidden for so many years, the Light is finding its way into the roots of the past, freeing this life from repetition and redundancy. What I thought I was, I no longer am.

As a child, I was empathetic and would feel misunderstood. As a young adult, I always sensed a barrier I needed to cross, a veil obscuring what was true. I tried many different methods to get through, and at times, I would, but the barrier always reappeared, and I would experience myself as separate again. This repetition had its place because, without it, I would not have been able to grasp the significance of these inner barriers. They were my inner barriers to perceiving and knowing the Self as the Eternal Self.

Life has given me many opportunities to see what "doesn't work," and my path has been about discovering these things. I've seen that personal effort can only take you so far and that surrender seems to be how we access the portal of pure potentiality. Through these many years of effort, failure, grace, and incredible inspiration, I have watched how the mind-body complex changes in the most profound ways, undetectable from the outside.

I have watched my mind trying to figure out how to be a better person to fit into its limited reality. I have gone unconscious for long extended periods when I believed that I needed something in this world to be a certain way, thinking that I would find peace when everything fell into place. Fortunately, nothing fell into place, and I was invited to question myself. When nothing that "I" wanted worked out, the separate self had nowhere to hide. This exposure of that self and its gradual dissolution has revealed a life without personal ideologies beyond intellectual understanding. And at times, a life without any clinging or resistance. That life is slowly coming to the forefront of my consciousness and is taking over. Yet, I do not know how many more illusions I will discover in myself. There seems to be an endless supply!

We are all here to grow beyond ourselves—beyond the separate self that needs security and a particular experience. The separate self needs security based on its beliefs of what security should look or feel like. I used "need" here versus "desire" because to desire security is only natural. But to think we "need" is based on our imagination of what it "needs" to look like. Need obstructs our relationship with "What Is." An unobstructed relationship with "What Is" keeps our process healthy and full of vitality, as it exposes every hiding place of the separate self and its programs. We begin recognizing "What Is" as the Sat-guru, the Beloved. When we can perceive "What Is" as a direct manifestation of the Beloved, calling us beyond our perceptions, we access a connection so potent and inspiring that it becomes a vehicle, a means to something remarkable.

We discover the door to true freedom as we become conscious of our familiar patterns. These patterns are nothing more than how consciousness is experiencing limitation within the mind-body complex. All we need to do is get *into* the familiar patterns and infuse them with conscious Awareness. This is the power we hold. Yet this seems challenging for many folks because the separate self doesn't like the familiar patterns and will develop many ways to avoid them. But when nothing else works, and we repeatedly face the same patterns, our ability to avoid them weakens. And when we cannot avoid our experience, we face all the parts that were never allowed into the Light. We learn to allow everything, infusing it with consciousness, which removes the inner, limited perceptions of separation. Awareness allows these deep psychological components because they are simply "What is." This moment is the door to freedom; and another door will open and reveal itself once we walk through the first one. Our past programs are our way into evolution, and learning to allow them is the most effective way to open beyond ourselves.

We all have an aspect of our life where we have a familiar pattern; maybe it is money, relationships, or health. It could be anything. We sense that things could be different. It is this inner sense that we need to pay attention to. It doesn't mean we know what "different" should look like. It means that there is some other possibility. Our inner sense is moving us toward something unfamiliar and Unknown.

The word "Totality" invokes a feeling that there is something other than what I am experiencing, so I looked it up in the dictionary. *Totality* means something total; it constitutes a total; the total amount, a whole.

The totality of consciousness includes everything imaginable and unimaginable, every dimension of possibility that could ever exist.

Every slight variation in this reality is included in every slight variation to every other reality and in everything that could ever be manifested as anything. The Totality I speak of is the Infinite reality that contains endless possibilities. So, of course, when you encounter familiar patterns and sense that things could be different, you are right.

Recognizing our familiar patterns and encountering them as consciousness—seeing them as "What Is"-is crucial. So, this is the paradox. To experience this reality in all its denseness is the way through it. At the beginning of our journey, we may attempt to transcend it all, and that's okay for a while. But we will keep encountering these limitations and frustrations because transcendence doesn't work forever. We are meant to access Totality through our bodies and nervous systems. This is where the perceptions of separation lie hidden.

Often, we go through years of trying to improve or ignore our patterns before we can even begin to get curious about them. The separate self doesn't like looking into the subconscious because that's where its deficiency lies. It sees them as something that must be hidden or managed. The separate self will make excuses, maybe even using spiritual bypassing to keep things hidden. The separate self can use anything in this world, including relationships, distractions, and meaningless identifications, to keep all that stuff unconscious.

Maybe we will get sick, so we go to many doctors. No one knows how to cure us; they may even tell us nothing is wrong with us. Or maybe we have financial troubles, and no matter what we do, we just can't seem to get ahead, and we fall deeper into debt. And then one day, through frustration and grace, we just stop, really stop, and let go. This moment of deep surrender, without self-judgment or feeling sorry for ourselves, opens us up to something *different*. At this moment, we are letting go of our cherished ideology, which dictates our experience. It is like telling God, "I don't know anymore, but you do. We ask for help and allow something other than our own will into the familiar pattern. We invite in *Universal Will*. When we love our process, or God, more than we need to feel secure, we can open and let go that much. We must let go so much that we lose all our ideas about letting go. At one point, we are open enough to have access to something *different*—the Totality.

Accessing multidimensional reality is within our divine blueprint. We are, by design, multi-dimensional beings. Sages have access because no one in their physiology tells them they can't. There are no more programs in them dictating limitations.

Amma has often shown me that she is accessing a multi-dimensional reality. There have been times when I have been on the edge, gripped in fear, and doubting my ability to continue. She comes to me and talks to me in her subtle way, letting me know that I am on the right path and that she is with me. There have been times when I have had some delusional thought, and Amma has looked at me right then, showing me that she heard that thought. This has happened countless times. All Amma's children experience this with her. Amma has given many of us clues about what realm she can access. She is like the mother hen showing her baby chicks how to access endless fields of freedom, whereas before, all we knew was the coop.

Our physiology is the portal through which we access the endless field of possibility. Within that Infinite Field are the means to help shift the 3-dimensional reality. The more open we become, the more freedom we feel in our nervous system. Our systems are transmuted through openness and allowing.

As we move into changing times, many people become confused and frightened as their 3-dimensional world changes. This is under-standable. But the more of us that can be open vessels for the Infinite reality to shift into something *different,* the more of a profound effect we can have. Our inner reality has a ripple effect through the Infinite. We are here to serve. We are pipes bringing light from the Totality into this reality, a reality that needs light. This is really service- service to the Whole.

The paradox lies in that we must access our familiar patterns all alone. No one can do it for us, nor can anyone even know what we are experiencing. As we go deeper into our illusions, there will be fewer words to describe what we are going through. We can try to explain it, but eventually, we will lose interest. We must learn to access our famil-iar patterns on our own. We must encounter our aloneness to develop the maturity to surrender completely. There can be only room for the Divine. We isolate the separate self when we embrace this type of utter aloneness. She has nowhere to turn to, no buddy to give her comfort.

This utter aloneness has an unprecedented potency because we keep all this Light and intention within; we do not expend it outwards. We are clear about the only thing that will work: aligning ourselves with the Beloved Totality.

At times it can be helpful to share our challenges with a spiritual friend as we lose all sense of the familiar. But spiritual support differs from relying on others to feel better about ourselves. Real spiritual support will open the door to the Unknown. The more we can let go of our dependency on others, the more effectively we will expose the separate self's needs. To encounter our aloneness is essential to accessing the Totality.

A true mystic is alone. That person has repeatedly met their darkness, which has deepened their relationship with God. They have repeatedly given themselves to the evolutionary process so that they have become steadfast in their resolution to go beyond themselves. They don't need to be recognized as anything special as that tendency has left their system. They enjoy their silent intimacy with the Divine so much more. And because no one knows of their silent relationship with the Divine, they are alone. They have often longed to share this intimacy, but they have recognized that only with another profound and mature mystic can they share what they feel. Because they have recognized that no one else can know their experience, they know aloneness, and they have embraced their aloneness.

The Beloved wants us alone. The Divine does not want to share us with anyone else, not in the way she has in mind. This does not mean we can't have friends or family; relationships can be a great way to see our patterns. But suppose we are holding onto our relationships for security. In that case, we will not surrender to aloneness (although we may be able to access aloneness through our failure to find security). We fall in love with the Infinite so profoundly and intimately that completely letting go of everything is possible through our aloneness. This is how we access total surrender, which is impossible in the early stages of our journey.

As we embrace our aloneness, we rely on the Beloved to be our most intimate companion, which doesn't give us anything tangible to hold onto. Our illusions become more obvious and easier to access when we have nothing to hold onto. We aren't leaning on anyone or anything else to help us go beyond ourselves. It is between us and the Beloved. This relationship is pure experience and very, very strong. This vital relationship makes us feel resolute so we can let go of everything else.

Our physiology may feel quite shaky sometimes; unsettledness happens when faced with the Unknown. Fear shows us deeper aspects of the separate self, giving us clear signs that we are right where we need to be. We may reach for distractions to help with the shakiness- people or things. But if the Beloved wants us alone, those things will not last.

Our minds may become kind of crazy at this level of aloneness. The brain is trying to keep us safe, and when there is nothing to hold onto, the mind can create looping, desperate thought patterns. The thought patterns are a manifestation of the brain perceiving danger. Learning to recognize this is very important. These thoughts may not have anything to do with reality, but these last attempts to find something are the last attempts of the separate self to hold onto itself. Allowing this to happen is crucial at this juncture. There is nothing wrong with your thoughts, so relate to them as "What Is."

We are entering the Unknown on a grand scale. But the most satisfying part at this point is having the Unknown enter our being. This fulfillment replaces any need to know. Our systems were made for this, and without the programs from the past being obstacles to embodiment, the Unknown moves in, deeper and deeper. It is a profound realization when we see this happening. It is direct seeing, the allowing of a pure reflection. It is like looking in a mirror, but there is no space between seeing and looking in the mirror. If this is happening in you, don't grasp it; let it move in.

The limited, separate mind cannot access anything other than what it already knows. But when the Totality begins to move in, it inhabits the brain. It moves into the neurological structure that dictates thought. Our thought patterns start to be influenced by this new occupancy, and we can experience vast expanses of profound silence. This silence has a profound effect on how the mind begins to shift its perceptions. We may notice that it doesn't care about things like it used to because it is starting to be free of the separate self's needs. The mirror begins to clear and to reflect the Eternal Self more clearly. The source of the mind is starting to shine forth.

When the Eternal Self is what is occupying and being reflected through the mind, we start seeing things differently. We are slowly beginning to see the world without any distortion. Before, we knew the world as an illusion. As Brahmin awakens within the mind-body complex, we begin to recognize that Brahmin "alone" is real. As the illusions are cleared from the mind, we see that the world is Brahmin.

As the mind begins to reflect, without distortion, we begin seeing without limitation. The mind is being influenced by Source, and when the separate self is absent and Self-Realization dawns, a new mind emerges. This new mind connects to the vast, unlimited nature of the Totality. The Universal Mind is unlimited, where it has access to all knowledge for the sake of humanity. This is how the great sages embody omniscient consciousness. When we recognize a true master, we recognize the power of consciousness within their mind. This is why they are masters; they access a reality beyond anything you and I know. This is why their company is so invaluable.

This is how real healers work. When Jesus healed, he didn't heal a sick person; he accessed a reality where that person was alive and well. He saw them as whole and healthy because he had access to that reality. He became a pipe for that reality to manifest in this one.

Many people will ask Amma for help with all kinds of things. Sometimes, Amma replies that she will make a Sankalpa, which is a Divine resolve. *San* means connection. *Kalpa* implies intention. A Sankalpa is possible because of its connection with the Totality. When we are one with the Totality, like a true master, all possibilities exist. Every little "problem" we encounter here has a solution in another world. If that solution benefits humanity, a Sankalpa can bring it forth.

We cannot access another reality just because we want to. Fortunately, it doesn't work like that. There is an intelligent design within our being, hidden within our physiology. Until we let go enough, that design will remain in seed form. That seed of Divine intelligence and infinite potential lies within the human species. Some seeds will sprout; others will not. Yet consciousness is there, within everyone and everything.

The True reality lies way beyond our minds, yet it is also closer than we can imagine. It is the only reality, but we have gone into a trance, thinking we are individuals with all kinds of needs, wants, likes, and dislikes. To go beyond all these limitations takes a great deal of intention and devotion. If we have intense devotion–a devotion stronger than our need to control–we can break the gravitational pull of the separate self. Devotion, impeccable discernment, and proper knowledge are the rocket ship that will take us beyond.

Anything is possible. It is up to us to find what takes us beyond ourselves. No one is going to do this for us. We must undertake the journey. We have within us the means to go way beyond the known. But Life is a quick, short trip, and it is over in the blink of an eye.

We set up a powerful intention each time we open to the Unknown. We must pay attention to what we think is true and what we think we know. When we see that we do not know, we let go a bit more. We must keep letting go, as this will open us enough for deep inquiry to be effective. In this way, the knower gets eradicated. Universal knowledge will remain out of reach until then.

Pure potential lies within everyone in seed form. The Divine Light of the Infinite is always here but remains dim. Slowly, the Light enters and makes its way through the vast nervous system, making room for itself.

Ultimately, the Infinite designs its own pipe. But only if it is allowed to.

25.
Epilogue

❧

2015. I am sitting by Amma's chair as Swamiji reads the note I have written to Amma. He reads it carefully, and as I watch his reaction, I can see that he understands the essence of my question. I notice him softening as if he realizes how difficult it must be for some of us in the West, away from Amma. We are in Santa Fe, which marks my 24th year with Amma. I have a concern I wish to tell her about, and I would like her to give me some advice.

My concern is that I lack self-confidence in the world. I have been back in the United States for 12 years now, and I have encountered a lot of failures. I have never known "worldly" success of any kind. All my "success" seems to be on the inside. And even though this is very important to me, I feel I am missing something. I feel incomplete. I have just finished writing a book and feel hesitant about putting it out there. I am uncertain whether I have the energy to market myself or the motivation to "try" to publish the book. And honestly, I don't feel confident in exposing myself so much. I don't want to fail again; I seek inspiration to keep going. My love affair with the Beloved still burns strong, but there is a gap that I can't seem to reconcile.

I have given Amma the manuscript of the book. She has it on her lap and is slowly looking through the pages. She is taking her time with it, looking through the pages and touching different sections here and there. It feels like she is reviewing the manuscript, even though she doesn't read English (or so she pretends).

Swamiji reads Amma the note. Amma then turns and looks at me, and with pure love radiating from her eyes, she strokes my face repeatedly. And then she starts yelling at me ferociously.

"Just do it!" she yells

"Don't even think about it!"

"All authors go through this. Just do it!"

"Don't worry—Amma will help you."

Her firm tone of voice goes right through me. It feels like an arrow piercing the core of my being. I am stunned by the power of her response. Our exchange happened so fast that I could not grasp what had happened. I want more from her—I want more guidance. Can she please tell me "How" to just do it? I don't want to get up. Amma and Swamiji patiently wait for me, but Amma has nothing more to say.

I reluctantly get up and return to my seat. I feel a little angry. Damn! Why can't she make it easy? She is constantly pushing me and pushing me beyond my comfort zone. She never gives me any instructions outside so I can feel more supported. Instead, it's always a push to keep going beyond everything "known." But I have noticed in the past that I seem to "know" the way, and I also seem to "know" which way not to go. My intuition, or even more profoundly, my instinct, is becoming more predominant. Amma is making me strong.

The answer she gave me was the answer I already knew deep down. It is a deep knowing coming from my essence. The answer tells me to "keep going—don't even think about it."

I have almost finished writing the book. For the last nine months, while writing, I have experienced a lack of confidence in how life will unfold. I have no drive to do anything except for the next step, finishing the book. Nine months ago, Amma told me to have people read it, so I passed it around and got some positive feedback. Maybe that was why Amma wanted me to have folks read it so I wouldn't lose heart.

And yet, there was such intense ferocity in her reply. It was a fierceness that was confident and did not doubt. She was bold and resolute about my process, which was already laid out. All I needed was to keep going with focus and resolve. I can feel her reply deep in my body. Just do it. Don't even think about it. Just do it.

I begin to feel a dream unravel, and within the dream, I see what is hiding there. It is the dream of a separate self, hiding in the story of "I need more self-confidence." I know the dream is just a belief since "I", the individual self, has never known worldly success. This dream that "I" lack self-confidence is the makeup of the separate self. I see that this belief was never fundamental to begin with. It does not exist. As this reality shifts, I feel a deep, familiar feeling. It is an ever-increasing and indestructible, deep inner confidence. It is a boldness that goes beyond words.

After I return from Santa Fe, this peeling back of the dream continues. The hiding places of insecurity and doubt keep showing up–they are weaker now but still there. In little thoughts, they float through, waiting to be seen and exposed to what they are; they hide places of a separate self. I feel like a big spotlight; I am exposing limitations and setting life free. This freeing up of life occurs in the body/mind/ nervous system, where the belief "I need more confidence" hides in increasingly subtle layers.

What keeps moving me beyond myself is an inner impulse towards freedom. This impulse has been with me for a very long time, for as long as I can remember. I have recognized that this impulse is also within all of life, within everyone.

Of course, there have been times when I have interpreted this impulse for freedom to mean something or to look like something. But the more transparent I become; this impulse feels like freedom itself. It is the freedom to go through all hiding places within and not hold onto any experience that looks like "awakening." It has the courage and the freedom to move through all limitations, all insecurity, and all feelings of separation. This impulse is freedom, moving into its capacity to expose all that is not free.

This impulse has felt like a thread. Through all the decades of personal struggles, doubts, and fears, this thread has kept going. It kept going when I thought my life was over and when I wanted off this ride of life. This thread continued when I perceived my life as meaningless and didn't see the point in continuing my spiritual journey. This thread has taken me beyond all ideas of me and my life, and it keeps going. And as the thread gets pulled through the eye of the needle, all that is not free cannot pass through.

This impulse towards freedom is not just a thread. It is life itself. It has the potential to go beyond all limitations. It carries the seed for a new life that has never been known. It is a vast power, and it is also infinite Grace. The more aware I am of this thread and its impulse, the more I can let go to it. It is a profound inspiration to go beyond this separate existence into something new and fresh.

The thread keeps going. We follow its lead, feeling it guiding us – deep within our being. It can take us very far—farther than our mind can imagine. Its impulse is to free everything in our being and our life. But don't think about it. Just do it. And then we will become intimate with that which is already free. We will become a new, never-before expression of the Infinite, taking this life beyond anything that has come before.

Addendum

December 2024.

We may understand something, relate to it, and how it will work, but we have no control over the outcome.

There was a deeper stopping after I spoke with Amma in 2015 and gave a few people a copy of my book. I knew I wasn't ready to put it out to the public. It wasn't about the lack of confidence or the manuscript. It was about timing. The book got put on the shelf, and I never picked it up again. I forgot all about it.

And then, in the summer of 2024, a woman I didn't know reached out to me while seeing Amma on tour. She was the sister of someone who had read the manuscript nine years prior, and her name was Mollie. Mollie had read the book and, without ever meeting Amma, felt moved to see her in New Mexico. She told me that because of my book, she felt inspired to meet Amma and understood how to be "with" Amma.

Mollie then went on to see Amma in other places on the tour. At the Chicago program, Mollie reached out to me again. She introduced me to her friend, who, understanding the significance of my book, offered to help me publish it.

I was stunned by this news. It was as if a lightning bolt had struck me right at the "knowing" center of my being. Amma had come, and it was time to "just do it." Amma made her Sankalpa and "helped" me.

I was sure the book was obsolete in many ways because of all the growth I had experienced in the past nine years. So, I told my new friends I needed to go through the book, thinking it would need a ton of work, which I didn't feel much energy for. But as I opened the files on my computer, I began to feel the potency of the transmission within the pages where Amma had slowly touched them. The words still felt significant and relevant, even in my current journey.

As I worked through the chapters, I didn't see the need to change much. I only briefly elaborated and clarified some things, as I didn't want to dilute the transmission. I only used a software program to clean up the writing, as I didn't want an editor to change anything. So, this book is much the same as the one Amma had blessed all those years ago, touching and running her fingers through the script. I also recognized that I couldn't have written this book now, as the movement is different now. It had to be written when I was still in a "teacher" function, which I am not in now.

In this offering, it feels like time has collapsed. Only now am I in a clearer position to share it—through Amma's grace. As they say, timing is everything. So, thank you, Amma, for everything.

www.ingramcontent.com/pod-product-compliance
Lightning Source LLC
Chambersburg PA
CBHW070914120626
46546CB00001B/255